FIRST BIKE

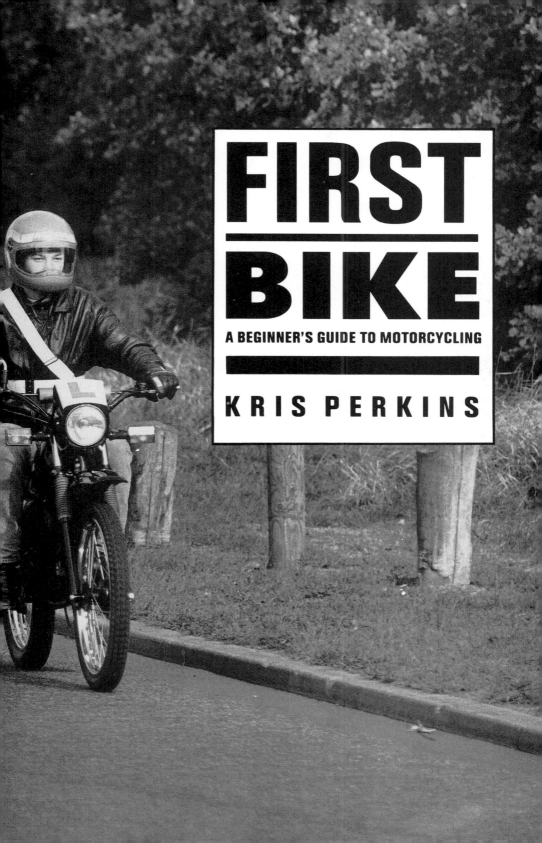

FIRST BIKE

A BEGINNER'S GUIDE TO MOTORCYCLING

KRIS PERKINS

Published in 1990 by Osprey Publishing,
59 Grosvenor Street,
London W1X 9DA

British Library Cataloguing in Publication
Data
Perkins, Kris
   First bike: a beginner's guide to
   motorcycling.
   1. Motorcycling
   I. Title
   796.7

ISBN 0-85045-971-0

Editor Ian Penberthy
Design Gwyn Lewis

Phototypeset by Keyspools Ltd, Warrington

Printed in Great Britain by
J. W. Arrowsmith, Bristol

Contents

Acknowledgements 6

Introduction 7

1 Before you start The learner rider 8

2 Legal requirements Documents Insurance Eyesight Highway Code Drugs and driving **10**

3 Battle gear Helmets Clothing Being seen **27**

4 Choosing your bike Choice Finance – Buying – Running **38**

5 Taking to the road Training Know your machine Daily/weekly checks **46**

6 Staying on the road The Part One test The Part Two test Reading the road Riding at night Security Cleaning Maintenance Luggage Pillion riding **55**

7 Help! Accident procedure Post-accident procedure **81**

8 Useful information Motorcycle rider's organizations Manufacturers Owners clubs Motoring organizations Papers and magazines Forms **86**

Glossary **92**

Acknowledgements

I wish to express my gratitude for the help and patience shown by my family and friends whilst writing this book; special thanks to Jean Wilson for her hours of typing, also to my editor, Ian Penberthy, and to Don Morley.

I should also like to thank the following individuals and companies for their assistance in the preparation of this book:

Andy Smith and Jeff Turner at Mitsui Machinery Sales (UK) Ltd (Yamaha)

Steve Kenward and Carolyne Walker at Heron Suzuki GB Ltd

Dave and Graham Sanderson at Honda UK Ltd

Peter Richardson at Kawasaki Motor (UK) Ltd

Screenflow Manufacturing Ltd

Watsonian–Squire Ltd (sidecars)

Mac at Nelson–Rigg UK Ltd (Fieldsheer clothing)

Vigen Vartivanien and James Theobald at Frontier Motorcycles

Alan Caddick at Lamba Autos

Freewheel UK Ltd (Sidewinder and trailers)

Controller of Her Majesty's Stationery Office

Department of Transport

Norwich Union Insurance Group

Mike Evans at the Institute of Motorcycling

Feridax (1957) Ltd (helmets and accessories)

Serval Marketing (motorcycle clothing)

Kate Goodyear (Bell helmets)

Datatool (motorcycle alarms)

Thetford Moulded Products Ltd (Centurion helmets)

Tony Holt, Chief Instructor, Kingston Star Rider

Ashman Brothers Ltd (boots)

Andover Norton International Ltd (security devices)

Castrol UK Ltd

Shell Oils UK Ltd

I & M Steiner Ltd (motorcycle luggage)

Sonic Communications International (intercoms)

Gary Aldridge (photograph)

Piers Dent (photograph)

Dave Rollinson (photograph)

Paul Willis (photographs)

Introduction

Motorcycling is one of the most exhilarating pastimes that you can experience. Whether you are riding on the road, racing around a track or skilfully manoeuvring across country, it will demand total concentration. You will forget life's problems as you enjoy the freedom and thrill of riding your machine. A motorcycle demands skill to be ridden well, and that skill is best learnt before you venture out on to the road.

Training is cheap for what you can get out of it—the knowledge and skills necessary for good riding, the opportunity to meet other people with a similar interest, and the challenge of learning how to control your machine in a variety of situations.

This book provides a wide variety of information for the first-time rider, but it cannot, nor is it intended to, replace practical motorcycle training.

A good rider is always willing to learn and never stops learning or trying to improve his or her riding. When you have been riding for a while you may like to prove to yourself, and to everyone else, how good a rider you are by taking an advanced motorcycle test. Only the very best ever pass this test, so it is a considerable achievement and something worth aiming for.

The fun of motorcycling (note that this photograph was taken using a trained, experienced rider)

CHAPTER

1

Before you start

The learner rider—The facts in brief

Age
At 16 you may ride a moped on the public road, as long as you have a provisional licence and insurance. At 17 and older, learner riders are restricted to machines of up to 125 cc, unless a sidecar is attached. In these circumstances, there is no limit to the capacity of the machine. Once you have taken and passed the Ministry of Transport Driving Test, you may then ride a bike of any capacity without a sidecar.

Within the next two years (by 1991), the provisional licence entitlement will change. It will only be validated on the successful completion of the new compulsory training course. The licence will then be valid for a period of ONE YEAR ONLY, and failure to take and pass the test(s) within that time will result in the suspension of the licence for one year.

Helmets
An approved motorcycle helmet must be worn by the rider at all times whilst riding. If a pillion passenger is carried, he or she must also wear an approved helmet. The helmet must be of the correct size and be securely fastened. The visor, or goggles, must also meet the legal standards.

Documents
The following documents must be obtained before you may take a machine on the road:
Insurance certificate or a cover note
The vehicle excise licence (Tax disc)

The vehicle registration document (Log book)
An MoT test certificate (if the machine is three or more years old)

Compulsory training
Within the next two years (by 1991), compulsory training will be introduced, covering both on-road and off-road instruction by government-approved motorcycle training bodies. All new riders will have to undergo the compulsory training course. At the end of the course, a certificate will be given to each learner who the instructor considers capable of riding on the road sufficiently well to be unaccompanied by an instructor. The certificate will only be available through schemes run by government-approved motorcycle training organizations.

L-plates

As a learner rider, you must display L-plates clearly at the front and rear of the machine. The regulation size for L-plates is 7 in. × 7 in. Special rigid L-plates, mounted on brackets, can be bought from dealers and accessory shops. The L-plates must not be cut down in size or wrapped around a fork leg.

Tests

The motorcycle driving test is split into two parts. Part One must be passed before you may apply for a Part Two test appointment. Therefore, you must pass both tests before you can qualify for a full motorcycle licence and remove your L-plates.

The Part One Test

The Part One Test is an off-road, machine handling test that you can take with a training organization appointed by the Department of Transport. This test will continue until the end of 1990.

The Part Two Test

Once you have passed the Part One Test, you can apply for a Part Two test appointment. This test is an examination of the rider's skill whilst riding on the road. It takes the form of a pursuit-type test where the candidate is followed by a government-appointed driving examiner, also riding on a motorcycle, around a specified route.

TOP The wrong way to mount an L-plate

ABOVE The correct way to mount an L-plate

LEFT The pursuit test

9

CHAPTER 2

Legal requirements

Machines

Mopeds A moped is a machine with an engine of under 50 cc and is restricted to a maximum speed of 30 mph. The only exception is a moped registered before 1 August 1977, when the speed restriction was introduced. Mopeds come in a variety of shapes and sizes.

Step-thru

Scooter

Trail

Sports

Commuter

Trail

Sports

125 cc motorcycles Learner riders are restricted to machines of up to 125 cc. There is also a power limit on the engine output, which the manufacturers have to state for their machines. Since 31 December 1982, this power output has been set at 12 brake horsepower (bhp). If your machine was registered before this date, it may produce more power, but it is still legal for you to ride it.

As with the moped, there is a large range of machines to choose from, one of which will suit you.

Sidecars At 17 or older, you can attach a sidecar to a machine of any capacity and, provided that you display L-plates and are insured, you may ride this combination on the road.

With a sidecar, you do not have to take the Part One test and, once you have passed the Part Two test, you can also ride any capacity machine solo.

As a learner with a sidecar, you may carry anyone in the sidecar, but only a full motorcycle licence holder may be carried on the pillion seat. There are many sorts of sidecars, some of which will carry passengers in comfort, while others are more basic; some are not even designed for passengers, but as stabilizers.

ABOVE A typical motorcycle and sidecar outfit

Trailers Motorcycles under 125 cc are not allowed to tow a trailer. With a larger capacity machine, you can tow one, but your speed will be limited to a maximum of 50 mph (60 mph on motorways) and the bike and trailer must be marked with their kerbside weight.

The trailer is limited to a maximum size of 1 m wide and 2.5 m in length, measured from the bike's rear axle to the rear of the trailer. Maximum weight is 150 kg, or two thirds of the machine's kerbside weight, whichever is the lower.

The trailer must also be fitted with both rear lights and brake stop lights. Passengers are not allowed to ride in the trailer.

ABOVE Sidewinder; the alternative to a sidecar

BELOW Motorcycle and trailer

Documents

If you use the roads, you must act responsibly towards everyone else who uses them. You need to be aware of the regulations relating to the documents required, insurance, the Highway Code, you as a learner rider, the machine, motorcycle helmets, accident procedure, drugs, pillion riding and eyesight.

Yes, this is a lot to learn but, as a road user, you have the potential to kill or injure others. The regulations are made to help and protect you, not to make life difficult. Some of these regulations are legal requirements, so you must obey them. It makes good sense.

Most matters concerning driving documents are dealt with by the Driver and Vehicle Licensing Centre (DVLC) at Swansea. There is a variety of forms, each of which has a code name. Basically, a 'D'-prefixed form relates to the driver, and a 'V'-prefixed form will relate to the vehicle or machine.

You need to use the correct form so, if in doubt, ask. Fill it in carefully and send it to the correct department. Note the postcode if you want to avoid delay.

1 Driving licence

To ride a moped or motorcycle on the road, you must first obtain a provisional driving licence.

Getting your provisional licence

You may apply for your first provisional licence up to two months before your 16th birthday. First obtain a D1 form from a main Post Office. This is green and white with the title, 'DVLC—Application for Your Driving Licence'.

Read through the form carefully, looking at the notes at the side of the form, and if you require further information ask for a leaflet entitled 'What you need to know about Driver Licensing'. This is form D100 and also available from the Post Office. When you are ready, fill in the form using black ink and block letters. Start with section 1, which asks for details about you,

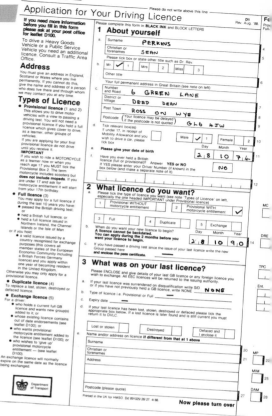

The driving licence application form

and remember to give your postcode.

In section 2, you are asked the type of licence that you want. If you wish to apply to ride a moped, you should tick box 1—provisional licence WITHOUT motorcycle entitlement. If you wish to learn to ride a motorcycle or scooter, tick box 2—provisional licence WITH motorcycle entitlement. Motorcycle entitlement group D (your licence group) will last for two years, during which time you must take and pass the Part One and Part Two motorcycle tests. If you fail to do so, you will have to wait 12 months before you may have a further provisional licence.

The date that you want the licence to begin will be the date of your 16th birthday if this is your first licence.

Section 3 concerns any previous licence you may have held. If applying for your

13

first licence write 'NONE' in part (a) and leave the rest of the section blank.

The fourth section concerns any driving offences that you may have committed. Make sure that you fill in this section honestly, as checks will be made and you will be prosecuted for making a false statement.

Section 5 asks about your eyesight. Do check that you can read a number plate at the given distance; if you cannot, go to an optician. If you require glasses or contact lenses to comply with the eyesight regulations, you must wear them every time you drive.

Further questions about your health are asked in section 6, and if you have any doubts about your answers to any of the questions, visit your doctor for advice.

Check through the form carefully before you sign and date the declaration in section 7. You can then send the form off, making sure that you send it to the correct address, noting the postcode, SA99 1AD, if this is your first licence. Make sure that you enclose the correct fee for the licence (do not send cash); a cheque or postal order should be made out to 'Department of Transport' and crossed 'Motor Tax Account'. (A cheque is crossed by writing across it the name of the account it is payable to; see the diagram below.)

When you receive your licence

When your provisional licence is sent to you, make sure that you check it carefully. Are all the details shown on it correct? It is important to check your address and postcode. Is the correct group of vehicles that you wish to ride shown? If everything is okay, make a note of your driver number on a piece of paper that you can keep with your other bike documents, and then sign your licence. You now hold a valid provisional driving licence, which means that, with insurance, you may ride your machine on the road.

You will also receive a copy of DL68 'Your Driving Test', which gives information on applying for and preparing for your driving test.

In the very near future, a provisional licence will only be validated on the successful completion of the compulsory training course. The licence will then be valid for a period of 12 MONTHS ONLY, and failure to take and pass the test(s) in that time will result in a suspension of your licence for one year.

2 Vehicle registration document

A vehicle registration document (once known as the log book) shows the registered keeper, that is, the person who keeps the vehicle on a public road—not neces-

RIGHT Clockwise, from top left: provisional driving licence, booklet DL68, vehicle registration document

BELOW How to cross a cheque

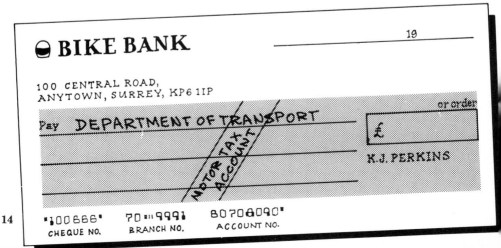

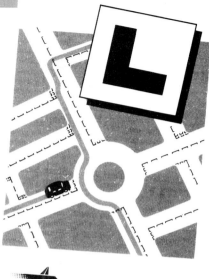

YOUR DRIVING TEST

THE DEPARTMENT
OF TRANSPORT

Department of Transport **P 3842855**

Vehicle Registration Document

V5
Rev. Sept/81

| Registration Mark | | 2 | Validation Character | **A** | 3 |

PLEASE QUOTE THE REGISTRATION MARK
IN ALL CORRESPONDENCE

Taxation Class	**BICYCLE**
Make	**YAMAHA**
Model/Type	**2-WHEEL MOTORCYCLE**

This is the Registration Document for the vehicle described opposite. The person named above is the Registered Keeper of the vehicle (the person recorded as keeping it).
The Registered Keeper is not necessarily the legal owner.
This Document is issued by the Driver and Vehicle Licensing Centre on behalf of the Secretary of State for Transport. Police officers and certain officers of the Department of Transport may require you to produce it for inspection at any reasonable time.
YOU ARE REQUIRED BY LAW TO NOTIFY CHANGES TO THE NAME AND ADDRESS OR VEHICLE PARTICULARS PRINTED ON THIS DOCUMENT AS SOON AS THEY OCCUR - SEE OVERLEAF.
For further information about registering, licensing, insuring and testing your vehicle, please ask at a post office or Local Vehicle Licensing Office for leaflet V100.

Colour(s)	**BLUE**
Type of Fuel	**PETROL**
VIN/Chassis/Frame No.	**202824**
Engine No.	**202824**
Cylinder Capacity	**73 CC**
Seating Capacity	
Taxable Weight	
Date of Registration	**23 01 75**
Last Change of Keeper	**17 07 85**
No. of Former Keepers	**7**

1. **PREVIOUS RECORDED KEEPER:**
   ACQUIRED VEHICLE ON 13 08 84.
2. **IF YOU SELL THE VEHICLE FILL-IN AND RETURN THE TEAR-OFF SLIP BELOW.**
3. **IF YOU ARE THE NEW KEEPER AND YOUR NAME IS NOT SHOWN ABOVE TELL US NOW BY FILLING IN THE BACK OF THIS FORM. WE WILL THEN SEND YOU A NEW DOCUMENT IN YOUR NAME.**

Doc Ref No. **5205 667 0197**
29 07 85

2721N069
862720

34

15

HGN 353N   **A**

The vehicle registration document application form V62 is shown with the following filled-in details:

```
... or in the Official Use area
... and CAPITAL LETTERS
... below

...
...vehicle          G  335  PGK          2

YAMAHA
3. Vauxhall, etc)

- WHEEL  MOTORCYCLE
Escort, Cavalier, etc)

vehicle   BLUE

...icle     BICYCLE
t Goods, HGV, Bicycle etc)

VIN number   2028246
a plate near the engine)


ddress of vehicle keeper
                            Please tick box or
                            give other title below
rs    2    Miss   3
r, Rev,
                                          9
ames    SEAN                              10
.KINS
  GREEN  LANE                             11
Sr  DEAN                                  12
S. ON  WYE                                13
ent may be delayed)   GL6  4JW
code is not quoted)

Registration Document for this vehicle in your name?
ES or NO   NO         Day  Month  Year
If NO give the date you  0,5  11  9,0   14
acquired the vehicle


1s
e Registration Document
given to me by the previous keeper of this vehicle

lost, stolen or defaced whilst in my possession

produced for other reasons
t above, what doesn't apply in your case).

turn the Registration Document if it is found, or given
vious keeper.

have checked the information given in this application
best of my knowledge it is correct and that the vehicle
to be licensed in accordance with the tax class shown above

S Perkins         Date  6·11·90

It is a criminal offence to obtain or attempt to obtain a
Registration Document by means of a false declaration.

check overleaf what you should now do with this form.
```

Official Use Only (V62):

```
VC  Post Office /       3
    DVLC use
        MKE             4
        MDL             5
        CLR             6
        TC              7
V10/V85/V70   L
    Proc
Independent   0         8

Post Office/ DVLC Date Stamp

CD      15      16
ISC         17
UW              18
DOW             19
SC      20
EN          21
CC      22
W/BT    23  F  24
AM      25
GW          26
DOP         27
```

The vehicle registration document application form V62

sarily the owner of the vehicle. The document gives the keeper's name and address, the registration number and other information about the vehicle. A new registration document is issued each time there is a change of keeper or any other detail.

If you buy a new machine from a dealer, they will normally arrange for it to be registered for you. Make sure that they fill in your name and address, including your postcode (this is very important), correctly on the registration application form V55.

When you receive the document by post, check that all the details are correct. If there is any mistake, send it back to the DVLC explaining exactly what is wrong.

If you buy a secondhand machine, the top part of the vehicle registration document should be given to you at the time of purchase. Remember that this document does not prove legal ownership. Before you buy a moped or motorcycle, you should be sure that the seller either owns the machine or is legally entitled to offer it for sale. Ask to see a bill of sale in their name or other evidence. If the vehicle is not registered in the seller's name, ask why. If there is any doubt about the ownership of the machine, do not proceed with the sale.

As soon as you become the keeper of the machine, you must inform the DVLC at Swansea. Complete the back of the registration document you were given by the seller. Do not wait until you have to re-license the vehicle to do this. If you were not given the document, you should apply for one, using form V62, which you can get from main Post Offices or Local Vehicle Licensing Offices (LVLO). The telephone number and address for your Local Vehicle Licensing Office may be found in the phone book under 'Transport, Department of'.

Unless you register the vehicle in your name, you will not be sent a renewal reminder form when the licence expires. Also, it may not be possible for the manufacturer to contact you if a possible safety defect is discovered on your type of machine.

If you lose your registration document, you should apply for a replacement, also using form V62. The DVLC will send you a new one after checking the application against the vehicle's record. If, later, you find the original document, send it to the DVLC with a letter of explanation.

If you change your address, you must tell the DVLC, using the back of the registration document. A new one will be sent to you free of charge. The registration document may contain details of the previous keeper. If it does not, or additional information is required, the registered keeper may obtain any available details of previous keepers free of charge from the Enquiries of Record Section, DVLC, Swansea, SA99 1AN. (Note—this is a different postcode to other departments.)

If you are unfortunate and have your machine stolen, you should report the

theft immediately to the police. They will automatically inform the DVLC on your behalf, so you do not have to contact them.

When you sell your machine, you must complete the lower half of the registration document headed 'Notification of Sale or Transfer'. Detach it and send it at once to DVLC, Swansea, SA99 1AR. The top part of the registration document should be given to the new keeper. Make a separate note of the buyer's name and address, and remind them that they must inform the DVLC at the same time.

3 Vehicle licence

A vehicle licence, road fund licence, or tax disc, is a receipt showing that you have paid the necessary vehicle excise duty for your machine. It shows the vehicle registration number, and until which date the duty has been paid. The disc must be clearly displayed on the left-hand side of the machine.

There is a range of tax disc holders available from motorcycle dealers and accessory shops. Few of these are completely waterproof, so wrap the disc in Cling Film or a clear polythene bag before putting it in the holder. You cannot transfer a licence from one machine to another.

Licences may be valid for six or 12 months. It may seem cheaper to buy two six-month licences, but you actually pay 10 per cent more than one for 12 months. Leaflet V149, available from licensing Post Offices and LVLOs, contains the current rates of vehicle excise duty.

Vehicle licence stamps, in units of £5, may be bought at any Post Office and used in payment for a vehicle licence.

By law, a vehicle ridden, parked or even left unattended on a public road must be licensed. If, for some reason, your machine is not being used on the road, it does not need a vehicle licence. If you do not have a vehicle licence for your machine and you use it on the road, you may be fined, as well as having to pay any back duty. The only exception is if you ride an unlicensed machine to and from a testing station for a pre-arranged compulsory MoT test. It must

ABOVE A road fund licence or tax disc. Wrap this in Cling Film to protect it from moisture

BELOW The tax disc holder should be mounted on the left side of the machine

Please DO NOT send this form to DVLC Swansea.

Vehicle licence application, V10

Except Heavy Goods Vehicles:
If you use a commercial or dual purpose vehicle to carry goods for business, and the vehicle weighs over 1525kg/30cwt, you will need to license it as a Heavy Goods Vehicle using form V85.

To help you

Poster V106   The amounts to pay for most vehicle licences are shown on poster V108 at Post Offices that issue vehicle licences and at Vehicle Registration Offices (VRO's).

Leaflet V149   Gives the amounts to pay for all vehicle licences.

Form V62   Application form for a Vehicle Registration Document — you must complete this if you have not got a Registration Document, even if you have recently applied for one but it hasn't arrived. You will only get one Document. You can get form V62 from Post Offices which issue licences and VRO's.

Leaflets V100 and V149 are available at most Post Offices and any VRO.

Don't forget these documents

☐ Registration Document
  If you haven't got one see 'Form V62' below

☐ Form V82
  you must complete this form if you haven't got a Registration Document — see note 'To help you' above.

☐ Insurance certificate or cover
  note not the policy, receipt or schedule nor a photocopy

☐ Vehicle test certificate
  if required

☐ Disabled exemption certificate
  for disabled tax class only
  MHS330, MY182 or MPB1266

☐ Payment
  see 'How to pay'

Where to get your licence disc

In Person   Take this application to any Post Office that issues vehicle licences.
  Your local Post Office can give you the address.

By Post   Send this application to the Head Postmaster (MVL Duty) at your nearest Head Post Office.
  In London you should send it to your nearest Head or District Post Office.
  Your local Post Office can give you the address, or you can look it up in the phone book or leaflet V100.

Exceptions   Send or take this application to a VRO if any of the following apply:
  ● the details you give in 'Vehicle details' overleaf are different from those on your Registration Document (but note that the 'Private' or 'Goods' taxation classes are acceptable instead of 'PLG' — don't go to a VRO if this is the only change).
  ● the vehicle is subject to a Customs concession or restriction.
  ● You require a licence disc for a 'Showman's Haulage' or 'General Haulage' vehicle.
  The address of your nearest VRO can be found in the phone book under 'Transport, Department of'.
  VRO addresses are also listed in leaflet V100.
  VRO's are open between 9.30am and 4.00pm Monday to Thursday, and between 9.30am and 3.30pm on Friday

How to pay

Payment to Post Offices can be made by:
  ● cheque or postal order, made payable to the 'Post Office' and crossed 'account payee'
  ● National Girobank transfer made payable to the Head Postmaster's account.
    The office where you pay locally can tell you the account number.
  ● cash and/or vehicle licence stamps. If you must post cash or vehicle licence stamps, please use registered post.
  ● the National Savings Bank 'Paybill' scheme.

If you have to get your licence at a VRO, payment can be made by:
  ● cheque or postal order, made payable to the 'Department of Transport' and crossed 'Motor Tax a/c'.
  ● National Girobank transfer made payable to 'Motor Tax a/c' in the credit account number box.
  ● cash and/or vehicle licence stamps. If you must post cash or vehicle licence stamps, please use registered post.

DEEP DEAN
ROSS ON WYE
GL6 4JW

Vehicle details

3 Registration mark of vehicle   G 335 PGK

4 Taxation class of licence required   BICYCLE
  If bicycle or tricycle, give cylinder capacity   73   (cc)
  If hackney, give seating capacity excluding driver   (seats)
  If showman's haulage or general haulage, give unladen weight   (kg)

5 Make and model   YAMAHA 2-WHEEL MOTORCYCLE

Licence details

6 State whether the licence is to run for 6 or 12 months   6   (months)

7 State date of expiry or surrender of last licence   19
  If you don't know this date because you first had the vehicle without a licence, give the exact date you got the vehicle   05 NOVEMBER 1990

8 State date from which the new licence is to run
  This must be the first day of the month in which you want the licence to start
  First day of   01 NOVEMBER 1990

9 Answer this question if there is a break between the dates at 7 and 8 above.
  Has the vehicle been kept (eg parked) or used on a public road at any time between these dates (other than for a pre-arranged compulsory vehicle test)? Answer YES or NO ....

Declaration

I declare that I have checked the information given in this application and that to the best of my knowledge it is correct.

I enclose the payment of £ 10   and the other documents required

Signature   S PERKINS

Date   06 NOVEMBER 1990

If you are signing for a partnership, limited company or other legal entity, give your position in the firm ....

VC
prefix
serial number
o/u payments
period
expiry month
SR
V5 changes
V62 noted

Vehicle licence application form V10

still be insured, however, and you should check your insurance details before doing this, as you may not be covered.

If your licence has previously expired, you may still ride your machine for up to 14 days after the expiry date, but within this period you must apply for a new one. You should note, however, that this 14-day period of grace is a concession. By law, a current licence must be displayed clearly at all times on the left-hand side of the machine (the same as the rider's left when seated on it) when it is on the road.

When you buy a new vehicle, the dealer will normally apply for the first licence at the same time as the registration document. Therefore, the machine should be licensed when you collect it. If the dealer does not apply for you, make sure they give you the application form (V65) so that you can apply to an LVLO yourself. Make sure that the details, including your postcode, are correct.

When you buy a used machine, the seller may agree to include the current licence with the machine. If they do not, or the licence has expired, you must use form V10 available from a Post Office or LVLO.

To license a machine, you will need to produce the following:

the registration document (with the changes section completed to show your name and address) or a complete form V62 available from main Post Offices and LVLOs.

the duty payable (leaflet V149 contains details of the current rates).

a valid certificate of insurance or cover note (not the policy).

a current MoT test certificate if the machine is over three years old.

About a fortnight before your vehicle licence expires, the DVLC will send a reminder form V11 to the address shown on the registration document. If you change your address, the form may still be used, provided that at the date from which the licence is to run, the machine details and taxation class printed on the form are correct. Without a reminder, apply instead on form V10.

You may apply for a licence up to 14 days before the licence is due to come into force, but if there has been a break in licensing of a month or more, you cannot be issued with a licence more than two working days before it is due to become valid.

A licence comes into force on the day of issue, but if you take it out in advance, it comes into force on the first day of the following month.

Normally, you can apply in person to a licence-issuing Post Office, but read the notes on the application form first. If you cannot get to the Post Office, you may apply by post to the Post Office listed on the form. Do not post applications to the DVLC.

Sometimes a vehicle licence may be lost, stolen, destroyed, mutilated or damaged. To replace it, you should apply for a duplicate, using form V20, which is available from licensing Post Offices and LVLOs. Your application and the fee payable should be sent, or taken, to an LVLO. If the vehicle is registered in your name, the LVLO will normally send you a temporary duplicate licence valid for a limited time. This allows them to check your application with DVLC records. If the machine is registered in your name and a licence is still in force, you will receive a duplicate, covering the full licence period.

You may also apply to the Duplicate Licensing Section, DVLC, Swansea, SA99 1AG, but in this case a temporary duplicate licence will not be issued. The fee and registration document must be sent with the application.

It is possible to obtain a refund on a vehicle licence if you stop using the vehicle. Refunds are only made for complete calendar months still to run, and a month will only count for a refund if the application is posted, or handed in at an LVLO, before the first day of the month. A refund cannot be back-dated. You should use form V14, which you can get from a Post Office that issues vehicle licences, and from LVLOs, or send the licence to the Refund

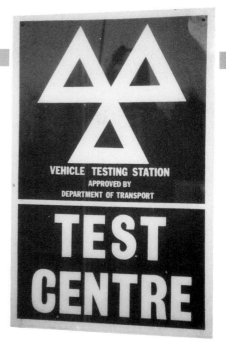

MoT testing stations display this sign

Section, DVLC, Swansea, SA99 1A1 (not to the Post Office).

You may apply for a refund even if you have lost your licence disc, or your machine has been stolen. A special application form, V33, is available from LVLOs.

4 MoT certificate

To prevent potentially dangerous machines being used on the roads, those over three years old must have a valid Vehicle Test (MoT) certificate. The age of the machine is calculated from the date of first registration shown on the registration document. If the machine was not new when first registered, the age is measured from the end of the year of manufacture.

It is illegal to use any machine that is subject to this test on the roads unless a valid test certificate is in force. If you are stopped and asked to produce the certificate by a police officer, you may be fined if you do not have one.

You must produce a valid test certificate when applying for a vehicle licence if the machine requires one. The vehicle licence renewal form, sent to you by the DVLC will remind you whether or not a certificate is needed.

The test is carried out by Department of the Environment authorized dealers, who

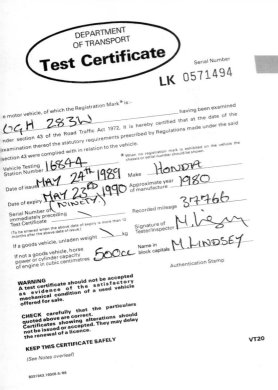

DEPARTMENT
OF TRANSPORT

Test Certificate

Serial Number

LK 0571494

...e motor vehicle, of which the Registration Mark* is:-

having been examined

0GH 283W

...nder section 43 of the Road Traffic Act 1972, it is hereby certified that at the date of the
...examination thereof the statutory requirements prescribed by Regulations made under the said
section 43 were complied with in relation to the vehicle.

* When no registration mark is exhibited on the vehicle the
chassis or serial number should be shown.

Vehicle Testing Station Number 16844

Date of issue MAY 24th 1989   Make HONDA

Date of expiry MAY 23rd 1990   Approximate year of manufacture 1980

Serial Number of immediately preceding Test Certificate
(To be entered when the above date of expiry is more than 12 months after the above date of issue.)

Recorded mileage 37766

Signature of Tester/Inspector M. Lindsey

Name in block capitals M. LINDSEY

If a goods vehicle, unladen weight _____ kg

If not a goods vehicle, horse power or cylinder capacity of engine in cubic centimetres 500cc

Authentication Stamp

WARNING
A test certificate should not be accepted
as evidence of the satisfactory
mechanical condition of a used vehicle
offered for sale.

CHECK carefully that the particulars
quoted above are correct.
Certificates showing alterations should
not be issued or accepted. They may delay
the renewal of a licence.

KEEP THIS CERTIFICATE SAFELY

(See Notes overleaf)

8031943.19306.6/88

VT20

Department of Transport   Motorcycle Inspection Report :
Road Traffic Act 1972 section 43   CUSTOMER'S COPY

Vehicle Reg. Mark____ VIN or Chassis no.____ Year of manufacture____
Make & Model____ Colour____ Recorded mileage____

A Testable Item	Inspect. Manual Ref. (see over)	Pass	Fail	Reasons for Failure and Remarks
Section I – Lighting Equipment				
Front Lamps	I/1			
Rear Lamps	I/1			
Headlamps	I/2			
Headlamp Aim	I/6			
Stop Lamps	I/3			
Rear Reflectors	I/4			
Direction Indicators	I/5			
Section II – Steering & Suspension				
Steering Controls	II/1			
Steering	II/2			
Front Suspension and wheel bearings	II/3			
Rear Suspension and wheel bearings	II/4			
Shock Absorbers	II/3,4			
Wheel Alignment	II/5			
Section III – Brakes				
Brake Controls	III/1			
Brake Systems	III/2			
Brake Performance	III/3			
Section IV – Tyres & Wheels				
Tyre Type	IV/1			
Tyre Condition	IV/1			
Roadwheels	IV/2			
Section V – Sidecar				
Sidecars	V/1			
Suspension and wheel bearings	V/2			
Wheel Alignment	V/3			
Section VI – General Items				
Horn	VI/1			
Exhaust System	VI/2			
Sidecar	VI/3			
General Structures	VI/3			

B. Test Result 1 ☐ PASS Test certificate issued. No:____
2 ☐ FAIL, see below

C Notice of Refusal of a Test Certificate (see notes overleaf)
1 ☐ For the reasons shown in the above Inspection Report
2 ☐ Because the inspection could not be completed, for the following reasons

D Warning In my opinion the vehicle is DANGEROUS to drive because of the following defects

Authorisation Stamp

E Signed ____ Date ____
(Tester/Inspector)
Name (Block capitals)____ Testing Station no.____

YOU ARE ADVISED TO KEEP THIS FORM   VT30M (1/86)

ABOVE Motorcycle inspection report form VT30M

LEFT The test certificate VT20

display the official sign bearing three white triangles on a blue background.

The test covers the brakes, lighting system, steering and suspension, tyres and wheels, horn, exhaust system, silencer, etc. If the machine is up to the standard required, a pass certificate VT20 will be issued, along with a motorcycle inspection report form (VT30M). This lists all the items covered by the test, and it is worth keeping with the test certificate.

If a machine fails on any of the points covered, a notification of refusal of a test certificate VT21 will be given to you. This will tell you what was not up to standard and is in need of repair. The machine must then be repaired and retested. The retest fee varies as follows:

If the machine is taken away for repair and then retested, you will have to pay the full fee again.

If the machine is taken away for repair, but taken to the same or another testing station within 14 working days, half the fee will be payable.

If the machine is left for repair and retest at the original test station, no fee is payable, but you will obviously need to pay for the repairs.

If you genuinely feel that your machine is roadworthy, but you have been issued with a notification of refusal of a test certificate, you may appeal against the refusal. If you wish to appeal against any or all of the grounds for the refusal to issue a test certificate, ask for the form VT17, obtainable from the Test Station. Send the completed form and the relevant fee to Traffic Area Head Office within 14 days of receiving the refusal notice.

While you are waiting for your appeal to be considered, do not have your vehicle repaired, since any change in the condition of your vehicle in respect of items on which the appeal is based may prejudice the outcome of the appeal. If your appeal is successful, the fee, or, if appropriate, part of it may be refunded to you.

Remember that a valid test certificate is no guarantee that a machine may be safely used on the road. It is your responsibility to ensure that your machine is roadworthy at all times.

Information leaflet V100 'Registering and Licensing your motor vehicle) is available from the Post Office.

Insurance

By law, you must have insurance, to cover your liability for causing death or bodily injury to other people on the road. Insurance is one of your most important buys as a motorcyclist, and you should choose your insurance company and type of policy very carefully.

You can obtain insurance cover from a variety of places; insurance companies advertise in the motorcycle press, and there are branch offices in many towns for the large companies. Insurance brokers deal with many companies and, therefore, should be able to find the best deal for you. Alternatively your dealer may be able to help arrange your insurance cover for you under one of the new manufacturers' schemes. Take your time and shop around for the best deal that provides adequate cover at a reasonable price. Read through the insurance agreement; if you do not understand a point, ask. Check that all the details are correct before you sign.

There are three types of insurance policy available with a great variation in price, according to the cover provided.

Third Party (Road Traffic Act only)
This is the absolute minimum type of insurance and, as the cheapest, obviously only provides the minimum cover. By law, this covers you for causing death or injury to the driver of another vehicle, the passengers, any pedestrian, your passenger, or any other road user you injure. Any other claim made against you, such as for vehicle damage, must be paid for by you. Cover is not provided for accidents on private property.

Third Party, Fire and Theft
In addition to the Third Party cover, you are also protected against fire damage and if your machine is stolen. For most people with a secondhand machine, this type of policy is the best form of cover.

Comprehensive
This is the most expensive type of insur-

A typical insurance proposal form

ance cover, it covers the above risks and in addition, covers damage to your machine caused by accident or maliciousness. You are covered even if the damage was your fault. Most policies will have a 'Policy Excess' clause which refers to the amount that you agree to pay in any claim. The more you agree to pay under excess, the cheaper will be your premium. If you have a new machine, this is the type of policy for you, and if you have bought your machine under a Hire Purchase agreement, you will have to take out such a policy.

In an effort to provide a more economical service to riders, some insurance companies now offer special insurance, such as

21

'rider policies' and 'specified bike policies'. A rider policy is a type of cover that allows you to ride any bike up to your chosen cc limit, and a specified bike policy only covers you for the one specified machine. These limited policies can make insurance premiums a lot cheaper, but check with your broker that you are getting the best cover for your circumstances.

Eyesight

By law, to obtain a licence and be able to ride on the road, your eyesight must meet the minimum requirements which are:

To be able to read, in good daylight (with the aid of glasses if worn), a registration mark fixed to a vehicle at a distance of 75 ft.

Protect your eyesight with a good visor or goggles

SE 12 AN
AP 6 WT

This diagram, when viewed from a distance of 8 ft, gives an approximate test of your ability to read a number plate at 75 ft

Many people ride or drive with their eyesight levels below the legal standards because they don't notice that their eyes have grown weaker. For your own health and safety, have your eyes checked every few years. If you do wear glasses or contact lenses normally, you must always wear them whilst driving. Remember that when you take your Part Two test, your eyesight will be checked before you start the test.

Your eyesight is valuable, so protect it by wearing BSI-approved goggles or a visor each time you ride your bike.

The Highway Code

In this country, the main guide for road users is the Highway Code. It is issued by Her Majesty's Stationery Office, and copies are available from most good stationers, bookshops or direct from HMSO. For the address of your nearest office, refer to 'Booksellers' in the Yellow Pages.

The Highway Code is not law, but you should know what is in it and act upon its recommendations. When you take your Part One and Part Two tests, you will be asked questions on the Highway Code. Therefore, you can see why it is an important code to learn. It contains information for you, the motorcyclist, on signs, road markings, etc. Read the Highway Code and put it into practice.

Most of the basic information, rules and regulations that apply to drivers also apply to motorcyclists.

You must
Always wear an approved type of safety helmet.
Ensure that your exhaust and silencer meet the noise regulations.

You must not
Carry more than one passenger on a solo motorcycle. The passenger must sit astride the machine on a proper seat, firmly fitted behind the rider and with proper footrests. Park in a parking meter zone, except in a specially-marked motorcycle park.

Pillion riders must
Wear an approved type of motorcycle helmet that is securely fastened.

Traffic signs
Traffic signs are carefully designed to give information to you, the road user. They are divided into five main types:

1 Signs that give orders.

2 Signs that give warnings.

3 Direction and other information signs.

4 Road markings.

5 Traffic light signals.

The Highway Code

Signs that give orders
These signs are mostly circular, and those with red borders are mostly what you must NOT do.

School crossing patrol

No vehicles

No entry for vehicular traffic

No right turn

No left turn

No U turns

Signs with blue circles, but no red borders, are mostly compulsory.

Ahead only

Turn left ahead (right if symbol reversed)

Turn left (right if symbol reversed)

Keep left (right if symbol reversed)

Signs that give warnings
These signs give warnings of hazards or potential hazards.

Dual carriageway ends

Slippery road

Two-way traffic straight ahead

Two-way traffic crosses one-way road

Traffic merges from left/right with equal priority

Directional and other information signs

Signs on motorways are mostly rectangular with blue backgrounds.

Start of motorway and point
from which motorway
regulations apply

On approaches to junctions
(junction number on black background)

Route confirmatory sign
after junction

End of motorway

At a junction leading directly into a motorway

Signs on primary routes or major roads are green with white letters and borders, with route numbers in yellow.

On approaches to junctions

Ring road

At the junction

Route
confirmatory
sign
after junction

Signs on non-primary routes have black borders and writing. Local direction signs have blue borders.

Signs on non-primary routes
Black borders

On approaches to junctions
(a symbol may sometimes be
shown to indicate a warning
of a hazard or prohibition on a
road leading from a junction)

Ring road

At the junction

Local direction signs
Blue borders

On approaches to junctions
(where there is a different route
for pedal cycles this may be
shown in a blue panel)

24

All information signs are rectangular.

Entrance to
controlled
parking zone

One-way street

Priority over vehicles
from opposite
direction

Advance warning of
restriction or prohibition
ahead

No through
road

Hospital
ahead

Distance to service area with fuel,
parking and cafeteria facilities
(The current petrol price may be shown
in pence per gallon or litre,
or may be omitted)

Parking place for
towed caravans

Road markings

Like traffic signs, markings on the road
give you information, orders or warnings.

1 Across the road.

2 Along the road.

Traffic light signals

RED means "Stop". Wait behind the stop line on the carriageway.

RED AND AMBER also means "Stop". Do not pass through or start until GREEN shows.

GREEN means you may go on if the way is clear. Take special care if you mean to turn left or right and give way to pedestrians who are crossing.

AMBER means "Stop" at the stop line. You may go on only if the AMBER appears after you have crossed the stop line or are so close to it that to pull up might cause an accident.

These samples from the Highway Code are pointers. You should obtain your own copy, learn its contents and put them into practice.

Drugs and driving

Under the Road Traffic Act 1962, driving under the influence of drink or drugs is one offence for which you may be disqualified from riding. Most people are aware that it is wrong to drink and drive, but have you considered the fact that many people drive whilst taking medicines?

Effect of alcohol Alcohol, a dilute poison made in many forms, is consumed by many people. In small doses, it produces a relaxed feeling, but it also slows your reactions and impairs your judgement of speed, distance, width, etc.

The introduction of the breathalyzer test has helped reduce the number of accidents due to drinking and driving. Any driver found to have a blood/alcohol level of more than 80/100 ml of blood faces prosecution, a heavy fine and the loss of their driving licence. To drink and drive is to be totally selfish to other innocent road users.

Effect of medicines Millions of people ride and drive having taken everyday medicines, but they are breaking the law, are you? If you ride whilst taking that cough syrup, or those pain-relieving tablets, are you fully in control of your machine?

It is common knowledge amongst doctors and pharmaceutical companies that most drugs impair your riding ability. If you are taking a medicine, read the label to see if it warns against riding. It not, ask the advice of your doctor or pharmacist.

Effect of drugs Drugs impair driving in three ways:
1 Direct effect.
2 Side effect.
3 Combination effect, if taken with alcohol or other drugs.
Taking any drug and riding is irresponsible. It is far better not to ride, but to wait until you have finished the drug and are in full control of yourself and your machine once more.

3

Battle gear

Helmets

The human body is not designed to withstand the damage that can occur in an accident, so protective clothing is vital. By law, the only protective clothing you must wear whilst riding a motorcycle is an approved type of safety helmet. Your head is important and should be protected as much as possible.

A human head weighs approximately 10 lb. If your body stops suddenly, from a speed of 5 mph, the head effectively weighs five times as much. At 30 mph, it weighs 30 times as much, or 300 lbs. If your head comes into contact with a stationary object at that speed, it has the same effect as being hit with a 300 lb sledge hammer. Perhaps you can understand why it is a good idea to wear a helmet.

How much you spend on a helmet depends on the old adage, 'If you have a £5 head, buy a £5 helmet.' Prices range from £20 to over £150 but, generally, the more you spend, the better the protection.

Types of helmet

There are two types of helmet—open-face and full-face—but there is a large range of styles and materials from which to choose.

For some people, the open-face helmet is more acceptable, as it is less claustrophobic. However, it does not offer as much protection as the full-face type and you will also require eye protection.

The full-face, or integral, helmet provides greater protection, but costs and weighs more. Eye protection, in the form of a visor, is usually built in.

A full-face helmet

Construction

Motorcycle helmets are generally made from one of the following materials, or a combination of them:

Fibreglass

Kevlar

Thermoplastics, such as Polycarbonate, ABS, or Ronfalin

Kevlar is a new, but expensive, material that is extremely strong and light. It is also used to make bulletproof vests!

A helmet comprises three main parts; the shell, an energy-absorbing liner, and a lining for comfort.

Open-face helmets

The shell

This is the high-impact-resistant outer layer of the helmet. It is also designed to slide so that in an accident the helmet won't snag or catch the road surface, causing bumping and banging of the head that could also lead to neck injuries. Shells come in many different shapes for both aerodynamic stability and styling. Choose a bright finish that will show up out on the road—white is the most visible. Vents, either for cooling or anti-misting, are becoming increasingly popular.

No thermoplastic helmet should be painted, as paint chemicals make the shell very brittle. This effect is not noticeable until the helmet is shattered by an impact. Stickers, badges, tape, etc, can also have a weakening effect.

Energy-absorbing liner

The internal liner is important for its energy-absorbing properties in an accident. This layer absorbs the shock that would otherwise be transmitted to your skull. Most helmet manufacturers use a liner of thick expanded polystyrene, a similar material to that used for packaging. You should never hang your helmet from the machine's handlebars or mirror, as you can easily compress the liner and weaken this layer.

The lining

The lining itself is to make the helmet comfortable to wear. Materials commonly used are brushed nylon, towelling, velour, crushed velour, velvet, etc. To help keep the lining clean, it is a very good idea to wear a balaclava to absorb sweat and the grease from your hair.

British Standards

In the UK, any helmet sold for road use must meet certain standards. The British Standards Institute is a testing body that tests the suitability of helmets to certain safety levels. Helmets are subjected to extremes of heat and cold, together with shock absorption, penetration and resistance tests. Any helmet meeting these standards will be given BSI approval and will carry the BSI 'kitemark'.

The current standard for helmets manufactured for sale after 1 July 1987 is BS6658. All the shell materials used at present for helmet manufacture pass the British Standards amendment 5. This was introduced as a test of the shell's resistance to petrol and solvents.

The new standard, BS6658; 1985, was introduced on 1 January 1986. This standard brings in new tests. It increases the severity of the tests on shock-absorption levels, the test of the strength of the chin bar, and the slideability of the shell, which could help to reduce neck injuries.

The last test on the helmet will be to assess the possibility of the helmet becoming detached from the head in the event of an accident.

The BSI helmet label

There are two groups under BS6658; group A is tough enough for racing or competition use, while group B is suitable for road use.

ACU

The Auto Cycle Union also endorses the standards of helmets with a silver or gold label.

The ACU helmet label

Snell

This American foundation imposes tougher tests than BSI, and only the very best helmets will gain an endorsement.

Helmet hints

Take your time when buying a helmet and find one that fits comfortably. Try the helmet on and fasten it securely, then try the following:

Hold the helmet with both hands and twist it gently to each side. There should be little movement in either direction.

Tilt the helmet forward and back. Again, there should be little movement.

Finally, try to pull the helmet off from the back to the front. If you can, you must try a smaller size or a different model.

Here are some more hints to help you:

Don't rely on the stated helmet size; judge by trying the helmet on.

Never buy a secondhand helmet, no matter how attractive it looks. You do not know how it has been treated.

Do not buy a helmet that has been sitting in a shop window. Ultra-violet rays from the sun weaken helmets over a period of time.

Spend as much as you can on a helmet.

Remember, the helmet can only protect you if it is securely fastened.

Always place your helmet on the ground, base down. If you place it on your seat, it will inevitably be knocked off on to the ground.

If you do drop your helmet, or you have an accident and the helmet is struck, even if it is unmarked, replace it. It's done its job! You cannot take a chance with a helmet.

Clean your helmet with warm water. Never use petroleum-based cleaners.

Visors can be cleaned with water and washing-up liquid.

To prevent misting, use a visor spray or, as

a cheaper alternative, a couple of drops of washing-up liquid polished into the inside surface. This will usually last about a week.

If the visor becomes scratched, replace it. Otherwise, it will produce a starring effect in bright light or when riding at night.

If you carry a pillion passenger, they should wear a helmet as good as yours with BSI-approved goggles or a visor.

Never have a helmet hanging on your bike by its straps whilst riding, as the turbulence will strain the fixing points of the straps and weaken them.

Replace your helmet every two years if it is thermoplastic, and three if it is fibreglass.

REMEMBER Look after your helmet, and it will look after you!

Visors and goggles

Eye protection is a must; an insect hitting your eye at 5 mph is painful, a piece of grit at 30 mph could blind you. Your eyesight is valuable, therefore you should take care that you use some form of eye protection whilst riding.

Since 1 July 1987, all visors and goggles,

These goggles also carry BSI approval

for both rider and pillion passenger, must have anti-scratch coatings and must not be tinted by more than 50 per cent. Approved eye protection is marked with the British Standards Institute 'kitemark' and the code BS4110ZA, or BS4110XA, or BS4110YA. The highest standard is ZA, and the lowest protection is indicated by YA.

If your visor or goggles become scratched, you must replace them. Any scratch will give a dazzling star effect at night with oncoming lights.

Anti-mist

Misting on the inside of the visor or goggles is a common problem in cold or wet weather. This reduces your vision, making life very dangerous.

It is easily cured by rubbing a few drops of washing-up liquid on to the inner surface of the visor or goggles. Gently polish the liquid until the surface is clear.

Anti-mist sprays are also available, but do check that they are suitable for use on your visor or goggles.

When riding; try not to rub your visor or goggles, since any airborne particles of grit will cause scratching. Occasionally check the mountings of your visor and tighten gently, if necessary.

NEVER RIDE WITHOUT EYE PROTECTION; EYES ARE TOO EASILY DAMAGED.

The markings on a BSI-approved visor

Practical riding

Clothing

Apart from wearing an approved type of motorcycle helmet, there is no law to say what you should wear whilst riding a moped or motorcycle. Remember, though, that your skin does not resist abrasion very well. Imagine sliding down the road on your hands and knees. Without protection, your skin would quickly wear away down to the bone. If you ride a bike, or sit

TOP View through a clean, unmarked visor

ABOVE View through a badly scratched visor

on the back, you must protect yourself. In addition, the weather in our country is rarely dry and hot, so weatherproof clothing must also be considered.

There are basically two types of clothing; protective and weatherproof. Some types serve both purposes.

31

LEFT Bright clothing will make you visible to other road users

When you ride in this country, it is very easy to get cold quickly, even during the summer. When you are cold, your reactions slow down and you become less alert. This could lead to an accident. Warm clothing will prevent this and stop you getting a chill.

Motorcycle clothing has become brighter and more practical in recent years, and there is an increasing range becoming available.

Whilst riding a moped or motorcycle, the absolute minimum that you should wear are strong trousers or jeans, a padded jacket, boots and a pair of gloves.

Protective clothing

The best material for resisting abrasion is leather. There are several types; goatskin, horse hide and steer hide. Other types of leather, such as 'nappa' or sheepskin, usually used to make fashion garments, are not strong enough and tear very easily. These should be avoided, as they will not protect you in an accident. Leather is not waterproof, so you will require waterproofs as well.

Waterproof clothing

Waterproofs should be totally effective in keeping out rain. There are few worst experiences than riding a motorcycle when you are wet and cold. The fewer the seams in the waterproofs, the better, as these are the weak spots where leaks often occur. When you buy weatherproof clothing, try it on over your normal riding gear and allow yourself a loose fit. If it is tight, you will weaken the seams and it will leak. It is also a good idea to choose clothing that is bright so that you can be seen when lighting conditions are poor, at night or when it is raining.

There are a variety of materials available:

Waxed cotton This material is cotton treated with wax to make it waterproof. It does tend to become dirty very quickly and will need reproofing at intervals.

Nylon This is the cheapest material, but nylon clothing has a limited life span.

PVC This is the most popular material at

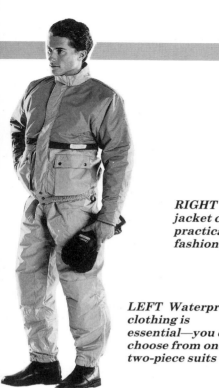

RIGHT A leather jacket can be practical and fashionable

LEFT Waterproof clothing is essential—you can choose from one- or two-piece suits

need to wear a thick jumper! Jackets should have long sleeves that cover your wrists when your hands are on the handlebars, and also be long enough at the back to keep you covered when leaning forward, so that there is no gap between jacket and trousers. Many jackets have zips to fasten them to the trousers. If not, it is easy to fasten strips of Velcro to the inside of the jacket and to the waistband of your trousers. This will stop any draught.

present, a range of unlined or lined, one-piece and two-piece suits being available.

Goretex This is a new material that is abrasion-resistant and waterproof, but it is very expensive.

If the label on a jacket, trousers or a suit states that the item is guaranteed to be 100 per cent waterproof, but it leaks, take it back to where you bought it and ask for it to be replaced.

Leather clothing
Leather jackets, jeans, boots, gloves and suits provide the best protection against abrasion, but they cannot protect your body from impact. Spend as much as you can and buy good quality clothing that fits comfortably when you sit on your machine.

Jackets
These come in a variety of styles and colours, but more important is the fit. Make sure the jacket fits comfortably over a thick jumper. Even in summer, you may

Leather jeans come in various styles

*One-piece
leather suits*

Jeans

Jeans are available in several types; normal style or with padded hips and knees, which are better for motorcycling. Salopettes are also available; the choice is yours. Do not buy jeans that are too tight as, when seated on a motorcycle, your legs will be bent and the circulation could be restricted. It is possible to have stretch panels inserted to prevent this.

Suits

Although expensive, two-piece leather suits are very smart and practical for road use. A good suit will be padded at the shoulders, elbows, knees, and hips, while a double layer of leather should be used for the seat panel. All linings should be of cotton or a similar material; avoid nylon, as it causes friction burns in an accident.

The zips on leather clothing should be treated with care and lightly sprayed with silicone at regular intervals to keep them moving smoothly. Never force them.

Out on the road, leather clothing will become dirty. It should be cleaned with a damp cloth and allowed to dry naturally. At intervals, apply hide food, which is available from motorcycle dealers, shoe shops and leather goods shops. This will keep the leather supple. Read the instructions carefully before use.

If your leather clothing does get wet, allow it to dry naturally and slowly. When dry, treat it with hide food. If you dry it by heat, it will become stiff and be useless.

Leather clothing is an investment; it will help protect you and, if looked after, it will last for a long time. If you cannot afford new leather clothing, it is well worth looking for secondhand garments.

Boots

Your feet are vulnerable on a moped or motorcycle, so you should wear the best protection you can. Trainers and fashion shoes give you little or no protection.

Leather boots that will protect your ankles and are high enough to protect your shins are best. There is a large range of styles to choose from. Boots are not waterproof, so over-boots will be necessary. An alternative are 'Derriboots' motorcycle boots, which are weatherproof, but provide less protection.

The soles of your boots must provide a

good grip, both on the foot pegs and when you put your feet down on the ground.

Gloves

Gloves must be strong, but flexible so that you can operate switches and other controls precisely. The best are made of leather and extend over the wrists. Do not wear nylon ski gloves, as they do not provide any protection and, in an accident, friction will melt them into your skin. Lined gloves are the best for cool or cold weather, while silk gloves can be worn to provide an extra layer of insulation.

To keep your hands dry, the cheapest method, but very effective, is to wear washing-up gloves over your leather gloves. Make sure that they are large enough not to restrict your circulation.

RIGHT Boots should have soles similar to this

BELOW A selection of motorcycle boot styles

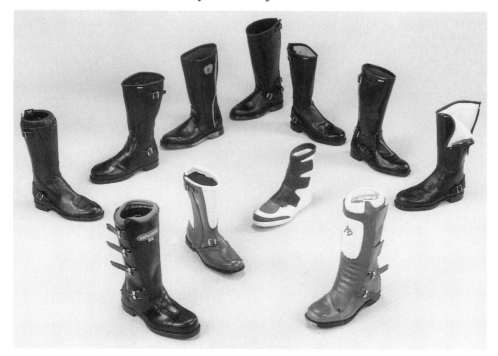

*ABOVE Regular
motorcycle gloves*

*BELOW Wet-
weather gloves*

36

Balaclava

A cotton or silk balaclava will keep your helmet lining clean and also keep you warmer in cold weather.

Being seen

Bright, light-coloured clothing not only looks good, but also gives you more chance of being seen. To supplement this, you can wear a retro-reflective tabard, jacket or sash and belt (Sam Browne).

The styles, designs and colours of motorcycle clothing are endless; choose the brightest you can, as it pays to be seen when riding.

Be bright, wear something light so that you can be seen day or night.

BELOW Wear bright clothing to be seen

ABOVE An example of a balaclava

CHAPTER 4

Choosing your bike

Choice

There is a large number of machines available for both the first-time rider, limited to a moped, and those of 17 and over, restricted to a machine of a maximum 125 cc, producing less than 12 bhp.

Mopeds
Mopeds can be divided into two main types:

The commuter/shopper type.

The sports moped.

Commuter/shopper
There are three main styles for these mopeds; the scooter type, the step-thru and the commuter.

These machines are relatively cheap to buy and insure, and are economical to run.

ABOVE Step-thru moped

Scooter

Commuter

Sports moped

For many, the appeal of a first machine will lie in either the trail type or sports roadster styling. These machines tend to be more expensive and, as a result, insurance premiums will be higher.

REMEMBER that good looks come at a price, and economy drops as these machines do fewer miles to the gallon than their more mundane looking cousins.

ABOVE Trail bike

LEFT Sports roadster

39

Learner 125 cc machines

From the age of 17, the law allows you to ride a machine up to a maximum of 125 cc.

Between 50 cc and 125 cc, the manufacturers offer a similar range of styles of machine, plus the motorcycle. Engine capacities for the motorcycle may be 80 cc, 100 cc or 125 cc. These machines are relatively expensive, not just in purchase price, but in insurance and running costs too. With the bigger engines, the rider must consider such points as fewer miles per gallon and tyre wear.

The machine shown opposite is one of the most popular types of learner trail bike. It has a liquid-cooled 124 cc, single-cylinder engine with kick start, a six-speed gearbox, disc brakes at the front and rear, and a weight of around 99 kg. The machine comes with indicators, mirrors, a rear carrier and a 9.3 litre tank.

Fuel consumption is around 55 mpg, and top speed is 71 mph.

The bike below is one of the fastest types of sports-restricted learner machine. It has a kick-start, 124 cc, liquid-cooled, two-stroke, single-cylinder engine, six-speed gearbox, front disc brake, rear drum brake,

RIGHT 124 cc trail bike

BELOW A 124 cc sports machine (restricted)

and a weight of approximately 94 kg (207 lb). This machine comes with dualseat (720 mm/28 in. high), indicators, mirrors, a fairing and a fuel capacity of 13 litres (2.9 gallons).

Fuel consumption is around 57 mpg, and the top speed 80 mph.

With such a wide choice of machines, you must first decide what you want the machine for. Can you afford to buy it, plus helmet, clothing, etc? Can you afford to insure it for its true value?

If possible, talk to the owners of bikes similar to the one in which you are interested. Find out its good points; has it any bad points?

Can you physically handle the machine, put it on and take if off its main stand? Are you able to push the machine around in a circle and manoeuvre it?

There are a lot of points to be considered when buying a machine, but it is a major decision. So, consider all the above and take your time; it's your choice!

Finance

The best way of buying a bike is to pay for it with cash, which means that you can shop around for the best deal. Few of us, however, can afford to do this and, therefore, have to raise the finance by other methods. This might be by one of the following:

Borrow from family or friends.
Bank loan.
Finance company.
Manufacturer/dealer finance.
Credit card.
Hire purchase.
Bank overdraft.
Credit broker.

When borrowing money from sources other than family or friends, you will be charged interest. This means that when you borrow a certain amount of money, you will be charged for the loan. The interest charge will vary, depending upon the length of time chosen for paying the money back and the amount borrowed.

Bank
The best way of borrowing money for a machine is by a personal loan from a bank. If you have a bank account, talk to your bank manager about a personal loan. Banks will usually lend you the money if you are over 18 and have a steady job.

Loans are normally repaid over a period from 12 to 36 months. The longer the period of time, the more you will be charged.

Finance company
The finance companies operate on a similar basis to the banks. The drawback is that their interest rates are usually higher.

Manufacturers/dealers
Sometimes, the manufacturers and dealers arrange deals on certain machines, such as interest-free credit. This means that you only pay back the actual cost of the loan. It is often possible to buy your bike, clothing, insurance and tax all at once by this means.

This offer is usually only available to you if you are over the age of 21. If you are under 21, it is still possible to make this deal, but you will need a guarantor.

A guarantor is someone, usually a parent or guardian, who agrees to ensure that the loan will be repaid and, if necessary, pay back the loan themselves.

Most credit dealers will insist that you take out insurance to cover the repayment of your loan. This means that your loan will be repaid if you lose your job or are unable to repay it due to other reasons.

In addition, you may also find that it is a requirement that the machine be insured for road use under a comprehensive type insurance policy.

Banks and finance companies usually produce leaflets that give details about loans and the total amount to be repaid for the set amount borrowed. These leaflets will also show the monthly repayment for a loan repaid over 12 months, 24 months, 36 months, or even longer. The figures may also show the cost of including an insurance policy for the loan.

It is now law that all advertisements show their rate or APR (annual percentage rate) figures. This will help you to choose the type of loan suitable for you.

Whatever type of loan or other method of finance, take your time in choosing, and read through all the forms carefully. If you are not sure of any of the points, ask your parents or friends for advice. Take a parent or friend with you when signing a loan agreement.

Running costs
Once you have bought the machine, you will need to budget for the following to keep it on the road:

Petrol
Oil
Lubricating oil, grease, silicone spray
Servicing—this will normally include the replacement, where necessary, of all worn parts, but remember to allow for such things as:
Tyres
Puncture repairs
Spark plugs
Bulbs
Cables
Cleaning materials
Additional security, i.e. a strong padlock and chain

All these are consumable, and it is important to remember that how you ride your machine will also determine how much it costs you per mile to run it.

If you ride sensibly and smoothly, you will get more miles to the gallon, your tyres and brakes will last longer and, therefore, you will have more money in your pocket.

Services should be carried out at the manufacturer's specified intervals. This will save you money in the long term and help you avoid large bills for repairs.

It will also save you money if you carry out the regular maintenance tasks specified in your owner's manual or handbook.

Time spent looking after your machine will help keep your running costs down.

An 80 cc scooter

Buying a bike privately

When you buy a bike from a private seller, you can often get a bargain, but you have to be far more careful than when you buy from a reputable dealer. A dealer should belong to one of the motorcycle retailers associations. Your rights of protection as a buyer in a private deal are not as great, nor is there a retail association to appeal to if things do go wrong.

The following points will help you when buying privately:

Decide on the type of machine and the amount that you can afford to spend and still have enough to buy a helmet, clothing, insurance and anything else that you need to get on the road.

Look in the local and motorcycle press for the type of machine that you want. Choose the adverts that give details of the machine and that are close to you. You will have to decide how far you are prepared to travel just to look.

When you phone, get as many details as possible: condition, mileage, extras, etc. It is worth asking if the seller will come to you, as this will save you time and the cost of a journey.

Always take a friend or someone you know who has a good knowledge of bikes. They will be able to look at the machine and help

you decide. Listen to their advice.

Do not just look at one bike; look at several, and if you are not lucky at first try again until you find what you want. Remember, many people sell their bikes at the end of the year, in the spring, and in June/July, just before they buy a new-registration model.

When you go to look at a bike, take a checklist of points to look out for and use this to inspect the machine from front to rear (an example is printed at the end of this chapter). Don't forget to check the machine's documents.

Never go and look at a bike at night. It is too easy to miss a major fault. Even with a torch or light, something may be missed.

Check over the seller—do they seem honest? Ask why they are selling the machine. Is the reason valid? If you are unsure of the seller, look elsewhere.

How does the machine appear? Is it clean from regular attention, or has it just been cleaned up to sell it? A close visual inspection all round will soon give you the answer.

Check that the engine and frame numbers are the same as those on the vehicle registration document. If they are not, do not accept any excuses and leave it alone.

Check that the speedometer has not been tampered with. Are the numbers scuffed? Is the mileage right for the age of the machine—not too high, nor too low?

Has the bike been crashed or dropped? Are the frame or forks damaged?

As you work through your checklist, mark down any fault and work out how much it might cost to put this right and whether it is worth it. Use this information to haggle over the price. Do not be embarrassed to challenge the asking price; the seller usually will have decided on a price and added a margin to this.

Who has done the servicing? If it has been done by a dealer, ask to see the service record book or the last service receipt. If the seller has done the servicing, ask for the routine tasks they have done. Their explanation should indicate the level of care the machine has received.

Ask the owner to start and run the machine for you. It should start first time and run smoothly. If there are any problems here, proceed with caution, as that pretty-looking machine may not be such a bargain after all.

Push the machine around in a figure of eight. Does it move smoothly? Listen for rattles and squeaks—if necessary investigate further.

If possible, and you have insurance cover, ask if you, or your friend, may ride the machine. Many bikes have been stolen by this method, so be prepared to leave your wallet or some other token, such as your driving licence, as security. If the seller, refuses, ask if you can be taken for a ride by them.

If the machine is three years old or more, it should have an MoT Certificate. Ask how long there is left on it, as its renewal will be an additional cost to bear.

After all this, do not forget to haggle.

It will be to your advantage to offer cash, but whichever way you pay, make sure that you receive the Registration Document and that it is correctly filled in and signed by the seller. Do not accept any excuse for failure to produce this document and, in addition, ask for a written and signed receipt that gives the make, model, registration number, colour and any other identifying feature of the machine.

A genuine seller will be keen to help you, but take care, for if you are unfortunate enough to buy a stolen machine, you will lose the bike and your money and have nothing to show for it.

The law states that bikes sold privately must be *as described*. If the seller says something about the quality of the bike, in front of a witness, and this later transpires to be untrue, you may be able to sue them in court for *misrepresentation*. This means that you could take your case to court to try to retrieve your money.

Checklist

Overall impression
Engine and frame numbers match registration document
Front tyre
Front wheel and bearings
Front forks; movement, leaks
Steering
Speedometer, instrumentation
Engine; nuts, bolts, screws missing/damaged
Any oil leaks
State of lubricating oil
Frame; damaged, rust
Levers and cables
Electrics, include battery, lights, horn, etc
Plastic parts; cracks, breaks
Seat
Petrol tank/tap leaks
Hoses; cracks or leaks
Unusual sounds
Suspension action/leaks
Exhaust; rust or leaks
Chain condition/wear limit
Rear wheel
Rear tyre condition and wear
Any extras

Buying from a dealer
When you buy a new or secondhand machine from a dealer, you are protected by three different purchasing laws under the code of practice drawn up by the motorcycle industry and backed by the Office of Fair Trading.

1 The bike must be of *merchantable quality*. This means that it must be suitable for the job it is supposed to do. A secondhand bike will not be as good as a new machine, but it must still do the job.

2 The bike must be *as described*—in any form of advertising or verbally by the dealer. Make sure it has all the features claimed for it. A new bike should be the

A 100 cc commuter

same as the one on display, unless it is made clear that some equipment is optional.

3 It must be *fit for any particular purpose* made known to the dealer. For example, if you say you want a cross-country machine, it is no good if they sell you a scooter.

If you think that your bike does not meet any of these requirements, take it back to the dealer immediately. You may be able to get it put right, or some or all of your money back or, if you agree, have the bike replaced. If you were shown the faults, or they were obvious, when you examined the bike before taking it away from the shop, you have no right to compensation.

Make sure that you choose a dealer who belongs to one of the four trade associations supporting the code of practice (see Trade Associations section for further details).

Secondhand bikes

1 All code dealers should carry out a pre-sale inspection of the bike. Ask to see their completed checklist before you buy, examining it and the machine closely. You should be given a copy of this when you buy. Any faults shown will be your responsibility, unless the dealer agrees to put them right.

2 If the bike's history is available from service records, repair bills, inspection reports and copies of warranties, the dealer should give you all the documents they have.

3 Code dealers must check that the bike's mileage is accurate; the machine's mileometer may be unreliable.

4 If the dealer makes any special claims about the bike, such as a reconditioned engine having been fitted, ask for this to be put in writing.

5 If a warranty is offered, find out what parts this covers and for how long.

If you buy a bike from a non-code dealer, you have full rights under law, but you will not be able to seek the help of a trade association if anything goes wrong.

The choice of dealer should be made carefully, with consideration of the following points;

The dealer should be as close as possible to where you live. Otherwise, if your bike is in for service, transport home could be a problem.

Are they close to transport services, like the bus station or railway station?

Are they a main dealer for the type of bike you want or have?

Are they service agents for the make of your machine?

Do they stock a large range of spares?

Are they helpful? If not, go elsewhere.

CHAPTER 5

Taking to the road

Training

If you take professional training to learn how to ride your moped or motorcycle, you will soon become a better, safer rider. Without training, you will learn more slowly, probably learning the wrong way, and certainly the hard way. Why make life difficult?

Training is relatively easy to obtain, especially through one of the national motorcycle training schemes, which have training centres located throughout the country. A phone call to one of the following will allow you to book a course at your nearest centre.

Star Rider
Federation House, 2309-11. Coventry Road, Birmingham B26 3PB.
Tel 021 742 4296

British Motorcyclists Federation
PO Box 2, Uckfield, East Sussex TN22 3NE.
Tel 082 571 2896

Royal Society for the Prevention of Accidents
Canon House, The Priory, Queensway, Birmingham, B4 6BS.
Tel 021 233 2461

Your local Road Safety Officer, whose number can be found in the phone book, usually under the County Hall or Local Council numbers, can advise you on the type of training scheme operating in your area.

Also, there are many schemes advertised in local papers and the motorcycle press, but be very careful to find out exactly what these courses offer. The 'big three' training schemes offer comprehensive basic courses that teach you all aspects of riding safely, the right skills and confidence.

Training checklist
Choose a local training scheme.

Book a training course.

Note the date, day and time of your course.

Arrange to have your machine delivered to the training site. (Your dealer will usually do this for you.)

Make a note of the address and check the location of the training site.

On the day:

Make sure that you and your machine arrive on time.

The beginning of the course

Make sure that you have a suitable helmet.

Make sure that you are correctly dressed and warm. Do you need waterproofs? Have you got your gloves?

Make sure that you have plenty of petrol and that the machine operates correctly.

Most dealers offer training as part of the deal when you buy your first bike.

What should you expect from your first training course? As an example, the following is a guide to the Star Bronze, or basic, course.

The dealer will usually deliver your machine to the training site for you. Make sure that you know where the training site is and that you arrive at the right time. The training site will be a tarmac area on private ground, so that you can learn to master your machine before you go out on the public roads with all their hazards.

When you arrive, you will be met by a qualified motorcycle instructor, who will introduce his or herself and then the rest of the training group. The course has a maximum of four trainees per instructor. You

Machine handling

will then be given a brief guide to the rules of the site, i.e. all riding must be done in the direction given by the instructor. This is followed by a check of documents, helmets and clothing. It is important to remember that the instructor is there to help you, so if you do not understand, or you want advice, just ask. As motorcycle enthusiasts, they will be only too willing to help with useful advice.

The first part of the Bronze course is designed to familiarize you with all the controls on your machine and to ensure that you know how to start and stop it confidently. Next comes the part you have been looking forward to, or dreading; actually riding the machine. The instructor will demonstrate clutch control where appropriate, and ensure that you can pull away and stop smoothly and safely. When you have mastered this, you will go on to braking and manoeuvring at low speeds, without putting your feet on the ground or stalling the engine. For some, this will be easy; others will need a little time to practise this. Relax and listen to what your instructor has to say. Remember, all motorcyclists have had to go through this experience!

By the end of the four-hour session, you will have learnt how to handle your machine, how to change gear (if you have gears), how to overtake safely, how to make observations, and how to give signals correctly. You will also be shown how to carry out daily and weekly basic safety and maintenance checks, such as topping up the oil level and checking tyre pressures. This may seem a lot to take in in just four hours, but because of the practical nature of the training, it is easily absorbed and you will soon be putting it into practice out on the road. The course is carefully designed to make you confident and competent enough to venture out on to the public roads, but this is just the start of your learning experience. The next stage is practical experience and booking a Silver, or intermediate, course to help you gain the skills needed to obtain a full motorcycle licence.

A B C D

E   F G H I J   K L M

Know your machine

A moped or a motorcycle is a complex piece of machinery, but with the use of its controls, you can make it perform a variety of tasks—start, move forward, accelerate, turn left, turn right, slow down, stop, etc.

The machine will only do what you make it do; the secret is to learn how to use the controls correctly. A good rider has total control over the machine, not vice versa.

Before you ride any machine, you must check it over, front to back, before you get on it. The locations of the controls do vary from machine to machine. Ensure that you know exactly where everything is and that you can operate them before you go out on the road. It is very dangerous to find that you do not know how to turn off the indicators when you are actually out there on the road.

Find and check the location on your machine of the following controls:

Make sure you know the location of your machine's controls and instruments: A, trip reset; B, speedometer; C, temperature gauge; D, rev-counter; E, clutch lever; F, oil warning light; G, neutral light; H, ignition switch; I, indicator light; J, high beam; K, lights; L, ignition kill switch; M, front brake lever

1 Front brake

2 Back brake

3 Throttle

4 Clutch (if fitted)

5 Gear lever (if fitted)

6 Petrol tap

7 Choke

8 Indicators

9 Light switches

10 Horn

11 Any other controls

Daily and weekly checks

For your own safety, and the continued reliability of your machine, the importance of daily and weekly checks cannot be over-emphasized. A neglected machine may develop a fault that could lead to the rider being thrown from the machine, or might result in a breakdown miles from anywhere. For these reasons, the wise rider gets into the habit of carrying out the following routine checks, both daily and weekly. With a little practice, the checks will only take a few minutes, but those minutes may save your life.

When you carry out your daily and, weekly checks, it is important that you make reference to the machine's handbook, or manual, for specific information. Please note that the following list is laid out in order of convenience, not in order of importance.

It is a good move to place your machine on its main stand and on a level surface before carrying out your checks.

1 Remove the fuel cap and check that you have sufficient fuel for your journey.

2 If your machine has a separate oil tank, take off the cap and check the level, or if it has a sight level, check this. If there is a sump dipstick, remove it, wipe it clean (on a lint-free cloth) and check the oil level.

3 Turn on the petrol tap and check for fuel leaks.

4 With the machine on its stand, spin the front wheel (you will need someone to push down on the back of the machine, or you will need to push up the front forks) and check the condition of the tyre tread and walls for cuts, etc. Check that the wheel and tyre run true (without any wobble) and that the tyre valve cap is tight. Repeat these checks on the rear wheel.

5 Take your machine off its stand and sit astride it, then push it forward a foot or two and test the front brake. With the brake still applied, rock the machine backwards and forwards to check for any movement in the steering head or in the brake action.

Have you enough fuel for your journey? *Checking the contents of the oil tank*

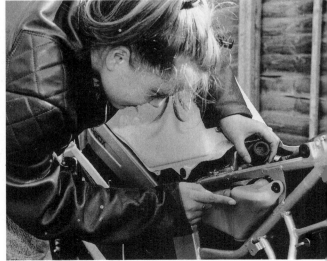

LEFT An oil level sight-gauge

BELOW LEFT The oil level dipstick

BELOW The oil level window

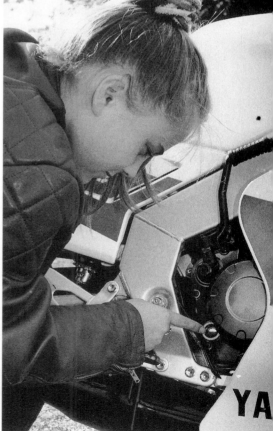

51

LEFT The petrol tap location may vary; make sure you know its positions for 'on', 'off' and 'reserve'

RIGHT Checking the rear chain tension (refer to the bike's manual)

BELOW RIGHT Check the operation of the steering

Remember to check the front brake, back brake and clutch (if fitted) cables for fraying.

Push the machine forward and check the operation of the rear brake.

6 Check the tension and action of the rear chain, according to the manufacturer's handbook, or manual. Adjust if necessary.

7 Sit on the machine and check the action of the front and the rear suspension. At the same time, make a visual check of the tyres for approximately correct pressure.

8 Turn the handlebars from right to left to check the operation of the steering. By placing your weight on the rear of the machine, the front wheel will be raised off the ground and the handlebars should require only a gentle push at the end of each bar to move them from lock to lock.

9 Push the machine forward to check that it is in neutral, then sit astride it, and start the engine. (Some mopeds must be placed on their centre stand first.)

10 Switch on the lights and check their operations, front and rear—high beam, dip or low beam and back light.

11 Apply the rear brake and check the operation of the brake warning light.

12 Check the operation of the direction indicators, if fitted.

13 Operate and check the action of the clutch, if fitted.

14 Where appropriate, with the clutch operated, move the gear lever to check its action and, where fitted, the neutral light.

15 When you have completed your checks, put on your riding gear and set off, carrying out the final check. Make sure that the road is quiet and then test the brake efficiency at 10–15 mph.

These simple checks will only take a few minutes of your time, but will help preserve you and your machine.

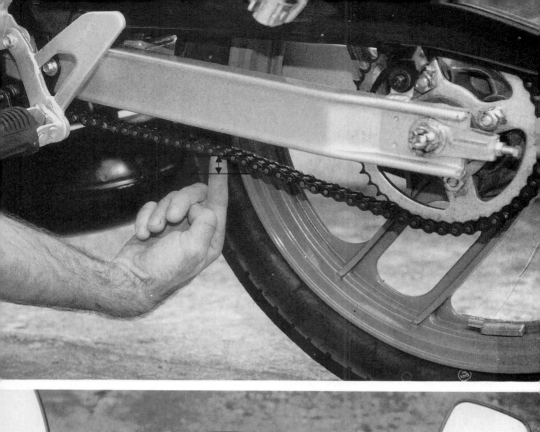

Check the action of the clutch, if fitted. It should move smoothly

Weekly checks

Once a week, time should be set aside to make a thorough check on your machine and carry out any necessary maintenance. ALWAYS refer to your machine's handbook, or manual, before making any adjustments. If you are unsure of any of the tasks, seek the advice of your dealer, do not take chances. Where adjustments are necessary, only use the correct tools, otherwise you will cause damage to your machine.

Make the following checks weekly, but refer to the maintenance section for further details.

1 Fuel tank; security of mountings and leaks.

2 Oil tank; security of mountings and leaks.

3 Oil levels; check engine, gearbox and transmission.

4 Levers and cables, lubricate and adjust where necessary.

5 Chain; clean, lubricate and adjust where necessary.

6 Wheels; check for damage, loose spokes or bearings.

7 Tyres; check the condition of tread, walls and correct pressures.

8 Battery; check correct electrolyte fluid, security of fittings, tightness of connections and cleanliness of terminals.

9 Nuts and bolts; tighten where necessary.

10 Greasing points; lubricate and grease where necessary.

11 Cleaning; clean your machine, refer to section on Cleaning.

CHAPTER

6

Staying on the road

To increase your safety and to help improve the standard of your riding, you should take further training and attempt your Part One and Part Two riding tests.

Within the next two years (by 1991), compulsory training will be introduced. This will include both off-road and on-road training. All new riders will be required to undertake the compulsory course with a government recognized training scheme. At the end of the Part One course, a certificate will be issued to each learner who, in the opinion of the instructor, has reached a standard considered good enough to be allowed to ride on the road without being accompanied by an instructor. The rider's provisional licence will be validated at this point. The rider then has 12 months in which to take and pass the Part Two test. Failure to meet this requirement will result in the suspension of the licence for one year.

The first test is a test of the rider's machine control; the second part is a test of the rider's ability out on the road. You must have passed Part One of the test before you can apply for a Part Two test appointment. When you have passed both tests, you may dispose of your L-plates.

The Part Two test system is a pursuit-type test. This means that when taking your test, the examiner will follow you, either by motorcycle or car, assessing your riding skills continuously during the test period.

Moped and sidecar outfit riders have a slight advantage in that they do not have to take the Part One test; they may take the Part Two test straight away. However,

if you pass on a moped, then decide to go on to a bigger bike, you will have to take a Part One test and re-take the Part Two.

The Part One test

The Part One course is designed to give the rider confidence in the control of the machine. The next stage is to develop these skills further and promote confidence whilst riding in traffic out on the road.

As an example, the Star Rider Silver, or intermediate, course consists of six two-hour sessions, structured to make the rider fully competent for the road.

Such courses prepare the rider for the Part One test, conduct an actual test and also prepare the rider for the Part Two test. They place emphasis on making pupils fully competent in all aspects of roadcraft.

The on-road training is undertaken on the public road with no more than four pupils per instructor and is followed by classroom sessions to cover aspects such as general safe riding, the Highway Code (you should have received a copy with your provisional licence) and the general theory of the course.

The following is meant purely as a theoretical guide to the Part One test. The only way to pass the Part One test first time is by taking training with a professional instructor and making sure that you listen to the instructor.

The Part One test comprises six riding exercises, and points are marked against you for mistakes made. If you total eight or more points, or you fall off, you will fail.

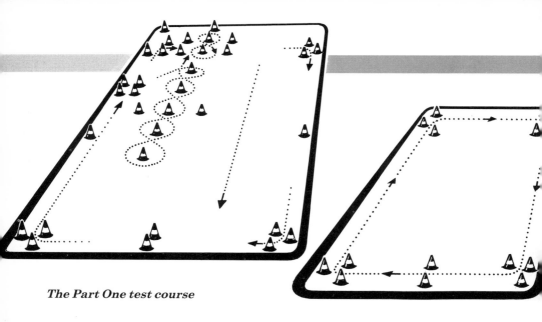

The Part One test course

Exercise one

You have to ride two anti-clockwise circuits of the outer cones. One point is deducted each time you put your foot down, start the bike in gear, use the controls incorrectly (stalling the bike, etc), go outside the manoeuvering area, partially lose control, or forget to look over your shoulder before starting off, changing direction or stopping. If you touch a cone, but keep to the correct side of it, you will be penalized two points. If you go outside the cones, you will have failed.

Exercise two

This is a repeat of exercise one, except that the circuit is in a clockwise direction.

Exercise one

Exercise three

You must repeat exercise two, but also stop and re-start at cones B. Points are deducted, as for exercises one and two. After exercise three, you can forget about the rearward observation for the purpose of the test.

Exercise four

This is the braking test. The idea is that you accelerate to 15 mph, then stop with your front wheel centrally between cones C. Marks are deducted for the incorrect use of the controls, not making full use of both the brakes, or stopping with the front wheel completely outside the marked area.

ABOVE Exercise two
BELOW Exercise three

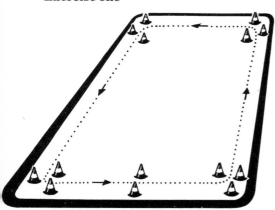

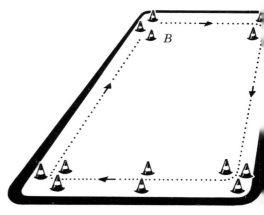

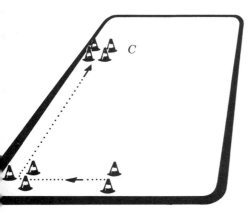

Exercise five
This is the slalom exercise, which requires plenty of practice. Remember to use the full width of the cones when turning to avoid ending up too tight. As with the other exercises, marks will be lost for putting your foot or feet down, or touching or moving a cone. You will also fail for going outside the area.

Exercise six
You are required to ride your machine in a figure of eight around the two central cones. Marks are lost as in exercise five.

Exercise seven
For this exercise, you have to ride in a straight line for 25 m whilst adjusting your speed to stay alongside the examiner, who will be walking and frequently altering pace—fast then slow, fast then slow, etc.

This is a test of the rider's ability to control the bike, the clutch and the throttle, and points are deducted for the incorrect use of these controls, or for putting a foot down, or too much wobbling.

The test concludes with some questions about motorcycling in general, and then you will be told if you have passed or failed. If you have passed, you will be given a

ABOVE Exercise four
BELOW Exercise five

ABOVE Exercise six
BELOW Exercise seven

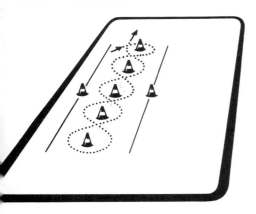

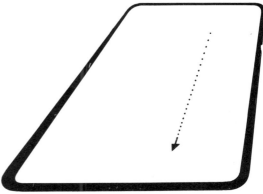

General Notes

Filling in this form

- Please make sure that you answer all the questions. Write in the white boxes using black ink and in CAPITAL LETTERS.
- If you find that you need more information to help you fill in this form, the booklet, DL68 'Your Driving test', provides helpful advice. Copies of this pamphlet are given out with provisional licences, you can also get a copy free from your Traffic Area Office.
- You can only make one application at a time.

Penalty

- If you deliberately give false information on this form you may be fined up to £1000.

Your driving test

- You should ensure that you are ready for the test. You can do this by seeking advice and tuition from an Approved Driving Instructor. Also make sure that you read the booklet DL68, 'Your Driving Test,' before taking the test.
- You must be legally entitled to drive and if you have got your driving licence (provisional or other) you should bring it with you.
- You must supply a suitable vehicle for your test:
  - It must not be loaded or partially loaded;
  - The examiner must be able to see through the rear windscreen;
  - It must be properly insured.
- If you cannot speak English or are deaf, you may bring along an interpreter.

Motor cycle test

- Part 1 motorcycle tests take place at Heavy Goods Vehicle driving test centres, these are given on the back of this form.
- If you are applying for Part 2 please make sure you enclose your certificate of passing Part 1 (form DL23). If you have lost your certificate you can get a duplicate from either the appointed training body or the Traffic Area Office to whom you applied for your test.

Table of vehicle groups

Group	Description of vehicles in the group
A	A vehicle without automatic transmission (e.g. a motor car with manual gear shift)
B	A vehicle with automatic transmission
C	Motor tricycle weighing not more than 450kg unladen
D	A motor bicycle (with or without side car)
E	Moped of maximum engine capacity 50cc.

- If you want to drive a vehicle not included in this table, see form D100 for advice. You can get this from the Post Office.

Checklist

- Have you answered all the questions and included your Driver Number?
- Have you filled in y...
- Have you signed a...
- Have you enclosed...

Where to sen...

- When you have ans... half down the dotte... filled in to the Clerk... where you want to... this form. Do Not s...

Important

- If you have not rece... inform the Traffic A...
- Please enclose eith... 'Department of Tra... write your driver nu... on the back. If you... counterfoil until yo...

Driver number   You must fill this in
- You will find this at the top of your licence

Name
- For title give Mr, Mrs, Miss or Ms.
- Give your surname and first name in full.
- For your other names give your initials only.
- Do not forget to sign and date the form.

Address
- If you change your address please tell the Traffic Area Office immediately so that we can contact you if your appointment has to be changed for any reason.

Test centre
- A list of centres is shown on the back of this form.
- For tests within the Metropolitan Traffic Area please write in the code shown (eg. Barnet — BT).

Motor cycle test
- If you are applying for Part 2 please enclose your certificate of passing Part 1, unless you are taking a test with a side-car

Type of vehicle
- See the table of vehicle groups and tick one box or give details of group in 'other' box.

Previous test
- Tick 'Yes' if you have taken a test before in the same vehicle group. If you have, you may not take another for one calendar month unless you are applying for a Part 1 motorcycle test.

Date
- Say when you will be ready to take your test.
- Tick any of the boxes to show any days when you cannot take your test.
- Please write down any periods (such as holidays) when you will be unable to take a test.
- Please tick 'Yes' if you could accept a test with less than a week's notice if one becomes available, otherwise tick 'No'.

Driver No. [ ][ ][ ][ ][ ][ ][ ][ ][ ][ ][ ][ ][ ][ ]

Title	MR	Surname	PERKINS	

First name & initials	SEAN	Date of Birth	day 2 8 month 0 7 year 4

Signed	S Perkins.	Dated	6 : 7 : 91

Address	6 GREEN LANE
	DEEP DEAN
	ROSS ON WYE Postcode GL6 4JW

☎ Home	STD code 01 234 5678	Work	STD code —

First choice centre	GLOUCESTER	Second choice centre	HEREFORD

Tick one box	Motorcycle test Part 1		Motorcycle test Part 2	✓

Type of Vehicle	A		B		C		D with side-car	
	D without side-car	✓	E		Other group			

Previous test	Yes	No ✓	Centre	Date	day month year

Earliest date	day 0 month 6 year 0 3 9 1

	Monday		Tuesday		Wednesday		Thursday		Friday	
Unacceptable days	am	pm	am	pm	am	pm	am	pm	am	pm
	1	2	3	4	5	6	7	8	9	0

Unacceptable dates	

Short notice test	Yes ✓	No

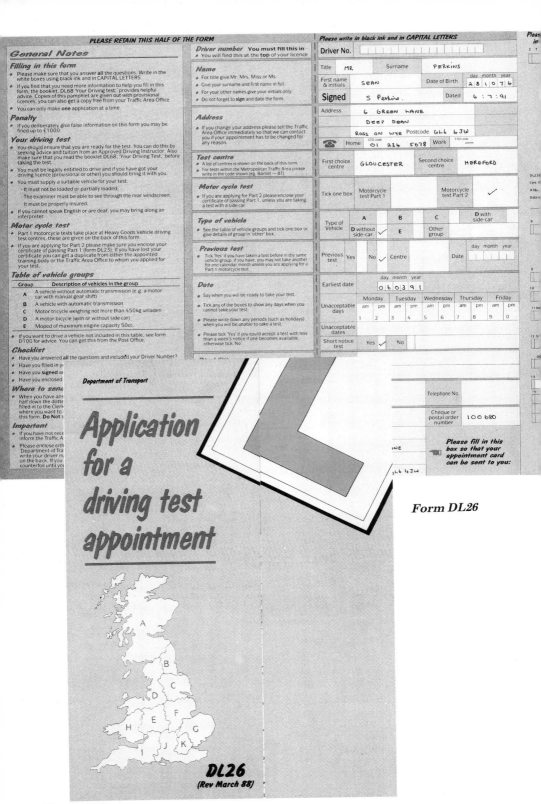

Department of Transport

Application for a driving test appointment

DL26
(Rev March 88)

Form DL26

Telephone No.	

Cheque or postal order number	100 680

Please fill in this box so that your appointment card can be sent to you:

Certificate of Passing Part One, form DL23MC. Training will help you get through the test smoothly and competently.

When you have passed your Part One test, you may then apply for a Part Two test appointment. Use 'Application for a driving test appointment' Form DL26, available from the Post Office. Remember to fill in the form correctly, enclose the correct test fee and your form DL23MC (the pass certificate).

It is always a good idea to get two forms in case you make a mistake. Read the form carefully first before filling it in, using a black pen and printing clearly

The Part Two test

After the Part One test, the real challenge is the Part Two or Ministry test. You have to convince the examiner that you are competent enough to be allowed to ride on all types of public road, including motorways; without the 'protection' of L-plates, under all conditions, and that you can handle your machine with skill, safety and consideration for other road users.

Convince the examiner of your ability and you will achieve a passport to greater excitement and freedom; you will be able to ride bigger machines, use the motorways and even carry a pillion passenger.

With these rewards for passing, the test is strict. It is carried out on normal public roads and is conducted by a highly-qualified Department of Transport examiner.

Test appointment
Having applied for a test appointment, you will receive a test appointment card with the date, time and place of your test. Check the details carefully. If there is any problem with the appointment, notify the Traffic Area Office (the number and address will be shown on the card) straight away and return your appointment card. You must give three whole days' notice, otherwise you will have to submit another

application form and pay another fee if you want a new test appointment.

NOTE. The three days' notice does not include the day that the clerk receives your notification, the day of your appointment, Saturdays, Sundays, Bank holidays, Christmas Day or Good Friday.

The test is conducted from a Department of Transport test centre, and you are well advised to visit the centre before your test to check the road conditions and find a suitable parking area.

The test
Before your test, check that you have the following so that you are not panicking on the day of your test:

1 Your test appointment card.

2 Your driving licence.

3 That your machine is fully roadworthy and that all the lights and indicators (if fitted) work. A clean machine creates a good impression with the examiner.

4 That you have L-plates clearly displayed at the front and the rear.

5 That you have an approved helmet and visor or goggles.

6 That you have sufficient fuel for the test.

7 Suitable clothing for the weather conditions, boots and gloves.

On the day
Allow sufficient time for the test; it usually lasts between 30 and 40 minutes. Add on your journey time and allow a period of 20 minutes for any delays.

Parking at the test centre may be difficult, so allow enough time to find a suitable spot close by. You should aim to be at the test centre at least five minutes before your test appointment time. If you are late, your test may be cancelled and you will lose your fee.

At the appointed time, the examiner will meet you, check your documents and ask you to show him or her to your machine. Outside, your eyesight will be tested by asking you to read a number plate on a nearby vehicle. You will then be given instructions as to the route to follow. The examiner will follow you around the course, either by motorcycle or by car, continually assessing your reaction to road traffic conditions.

Each test centre has its own pattern of test routes designed to take in most traffic conditions, such as left and right turns, roundabouts, traffic lights, etc.

When the examiner is satisfied with the number of circuits carried out, you will be stopped and asked questions on the Highway Code and other motoring points, such as when should you not overtake other vehicles, the traffic light sequence, etc.

You will then be told whether you have been successful and passed your test or if you have failed. If you have passed, you will be given a pass certificate and you may remove your L-plates. If you have failed, the examiner will give you a form DL24 Statement of Failure, on which you will

find the points on your riding that require special attention. These, and other points not shown, will be why you failed. The examiner is not allowed, nor will have the time, to discuss the test with you. You must then wait a full calendar month before you can take the test again.

Show the statement of failure to your instructor so that they can help you correct these main faults, in addition to your general riding. Obviously everyone's test is different, but this gives you a rough idea of what to expect on your test. Your training course will have prepared you, and this is the chance to prove that you can do it!

If you pass
If you are successful in passing your test, the world of motorcycling will be opened up to you. Remember, however, that having passed the test does not make you an expert motorcyclist. You will never stop learning on two wheels. To help you im-

Look for clues

prove your standard of riding, you can take further training and tests, but advanced motorcycle riding requires a book of its own and highly-qualified instructors to help you acquire the necessary skills. In the future, you may have learnt enough and be proficient enough to take on the ultimate two-wheel challenge; the advanced motorcycle test. Not many pass the test, as you have to be very good to impress the examiner, who will follow closely behind you over a 30 or 40 mile route, watching your every move.

Reading the road

As a motorcyclist, reading the road means more than just seeing what is in front of you. It means observing and reacting to what can be seen, what cannot be seen, and what could possibly happen.

Your eyes provide most of your information whilst riding. Therefore, it is a good idea to protect them and to have an eye test at regular intervals. By law, you must be able to read a number plate with $3\frac{1}{2}$ in. letters at 75 ft, or 67 ft with the new-style number plates. If you cannot, visit an optician for glasses or contact lenses; you must also inform the DVLC at Swansea. If you wore glasses or contact lenses when you took your test, you must wear them whenever you ride your bike.

Whilst riding, you must look both in front, up and down, from side to side, and also to the rear. In addition to looking, you must react to what you see. Does it pose a threat to you? Do you need to take any action, slow down, alter course, use your horn, or some other action? What is the condition of the road surface? Are there any hazards such as potholes, gravel, diesel, etc? What is happening in the distance?

A rider under test

By really looking, you can obtain advance warning of changes in road direction, the movement of other road users, and the approach to any potential hazard.

Forward observation must also be linked with sideways observations. Is that car going to pull out? Is someone about to step off the pavement?

If you are ever unsure as to whether or not you have been seen, use your horn to let others know that you are approaching.

Rearward observations are vital to let you know what is happening behind you. Are you about to be overtaken?

This constant eye movement demands concentration if you are to observe and react to what is happening around you. Observations can be linked so that you have an idea of what other road users may be about to do.

You must never make assumptions about other road users' intentions. The car in front may be indicating a left turn, but perhaps the driver has not cancelled the indicators from an earlier turn.

If you ride for a long distance, it is essential to stop after a certain number of miles, or period of time, so that you can

ABOVE Have you been seen? Do you need to use the horn?

RIGHT Watch out for the road surface

relax and have a short rest. By doing this, you will be able to maintain your concentration and, therefore, observations so that you can ride safely. A brief loss of concentration could mean that you will fail to see and react to a hazard. Do not ride if you are very tired or feeling unwell.

REMEMBER, road markings and traffic signs are put there for a purpose, to help you by giving you information. However, they are of no use unless you see and react to them.

ABOVE Observe from side to side   *BELOW Forward observation: road surface;*

seen you? What's round the corner?

Riding at night

At night, your ability to see and make effective observations will be drastically reduced, so you must cut your speed and increase your concentration. Night covers the period from dusk, when the sun goes down, to dawn, when the sun rises. There are official lighting-up times, usually to be found on the front pages of newspapers, but it is sensible to switch on your lights as soon as it becomes dull. Having your lights on in daylight will add greatly to your conspicuity; others will be able to see you and know in which direction you are travelling.

Your eyes take time to adjust to changes in light, so before you start a journey at night, wait several minutes to allow your eyes to adjust. You can speed up the process by opening and shutting your eyes a few times. To ride safely at night, it is essential that you ride only at a speed dictated by the range of the bike's headlight. This will allow you to stop in the length of road that is clearly visible ahead of you.

Your observations will be affected by the state of your visor or goggles. These must not be tinted at all for night-time use; any scratch will cause dazzle, so they should be replaced.

Read the road ahead. Look at the road surface, watch for traffic signs and road markings for information, and be aware of potential hazards such as unlit vehicles, rubbish skips, etc. A glimpse of headlights in the distance will give you an early warning of the approach of other vehicles. If your lights pick out the reflections from the eyes of animals at the roadside, slow down in case they run out in front of you. If it is raining, or the road surface is wet, this may cause distracting reflections, particularly where there are street and shop lights as well as vehicle lights.

By law, all of your lights must be in working order and be correctly adjusted so

LEFT Rearward observation

that they do not dazzle oncoming vehicles. During daylight hours, if weather conditions or light conditions are poor, you are required by law to use dipped lights.

It is important to remember that the range of your lights will vary from dipped beam to high beam.

Do not forget that, at night, it is very difficult to judge both speed and distance. Vehicles often appear to be further away than they actually are. Always keep a safe

TOP A clear visor is essential at night

ABOVE A scratched visor is dangerous

distance between you and the vehicle in front.

The power of the headlight is dictated by the output of your machine's generator. Clean lenses on your lights will allow none of the brightness to be lost, enabling you to see and be seen. It is a good idea to carry a

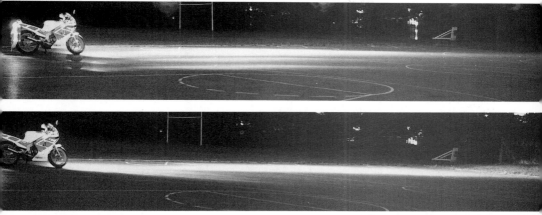

TOP Dipped beam

ABOVE High beam (Photos G. W. Aldridge)

Be seeen at night—wear reflective clothing

spare set of bulbs on your machine if you do a lot of riding at night.

Take care not to dazzle other road users with the headlight; dip the light when approaching other vehicles, both oncoming and when coming up behind. Do not do this too soon, as you will leave a blind spot where there may be a hidden hazard. Care should be taken to prevent dazzling other road users when approaching bends, or where the road goes up or downhill. If you are unfortunate enough to be dazzled by an oncoming vehicle, do not retaliate. Instead, reduce your speed and, if necessary, signal, slow down and stop. Let your eyes re-adjust before continuing.

Your ability to be seen by other road users at night, or in poor visibility, will be greatly aided by the use of reflective and retro-reflective patches, belts and clothing. Any reflectors, such as your number plate, or reflective strips on your machine should be kept clean to aid your conspicuity.

Do not give motorcycling a bad name through unnecessary noise at night, do not rev your engine whilst you're stationary, and do not use your horn in a built-up area between 11.30 pm and 7 am.

BE BRIGHT, BE SEEN AT NIGHT!

Security

Motorcycle theft is a growing problem in this country. It is sensible, therefore, to recognize this and take steps to safeguard your machine. Bikes are either ridden or pushed away, or loaded into the back of a van. Once your bike has been stolen, you might get it back a week later in a poor state, or you may never see it again.

There are a number of ways to protect your machine (some are mentioned below), but it is impossible to say which is the best. The manufacturers fit many of their machines with ignition/steering locks, but these are often too vulnerable, so you must use additional safeguards.

Security begins at home; try to park your bike out of sight, preferably in a secure garage. If you have to leave it outside, invest in a plastic or canvas bike cover, as this will hide the type of bike. If possible, buy one that has eyelets in it, as you can then put a padlock through to prevent the cover being removed.

ABOVE A shackle lock

BELOW One of the latest locks

Many bikes are taken by casual thieves who want a joy ride. They can be deterred by visual devices such as padlocks and chains. To be effective, you should padlock both the front and rear wheels. To do this, you will need around 2 m of heavy-gauge security chain, which your dealer should be able to supply you with, or look in the motorcycle press. Pass the chain around a solid part of the bike, e.g. the frame, and also loop the chain around a solid object, like a lamp post. If you are with other riders, chain the machines together, making sure that the chain only fits around the solid parts.

Shackle locks are extremely resistant to being forced and are now available. These can be highly effective in securing your machine.

In addition to visible deterrents, you can supplement your defences with a bike alarm from the range that is now available. The padlock and chain will put off most thieves, but if they still continue in their attempt to take your machine, the alarm should stop them succeeding. The prices of

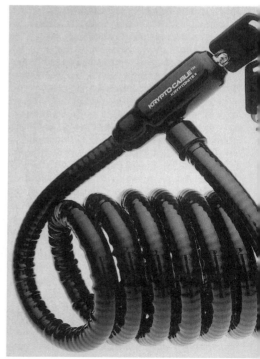

alarms range from around £20 to over £120, the cost being dictated by the functions that the alarm offers.

The cheapest consists of a movement sensor and an alarm signal generator. This alarm is simply bolted to the machine and is key operated. If the machine is moved when the alarm is set, the sensor will trigger the alarm.

The more expensive devices are far more difficult to fit, as they are wired into the bike's circuitry, but they offer more individual circuit protection if the ignition is operated, or if the machine is moved, or the ignition circuit is tampered with.

If you make the effort to mark the parts of your machine with security markers or by stamping or etching them with your registration number, it will help the police trace your bike if it is stolen.

Brand-new machines are very popular with thieves, so when you buy your bike, ask your dealer about protecting your investment. Do take the time to protect your machine, otherwise you might be without it for a very long time.

When you are out, always remember to lock your machine and leave it where it can be seen. At night, park under a bright light, as this should help deter would-be thieves.

ABOVE A machine secured against theft

BELOW An electronic alarm

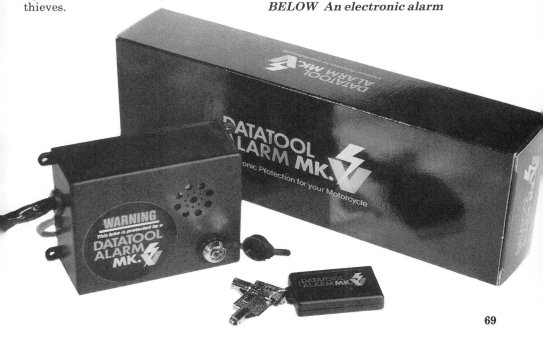

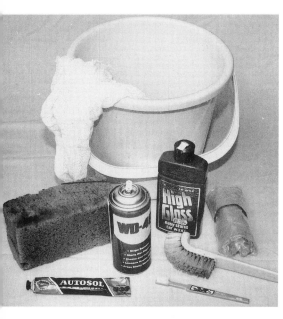

ABOVE A good cleaning kit

BELOW An old toothbrush is useful for cleaning in tight corners

Cleaning

If you keep your machine clean, it will look good and last longer. You will also be able to spot any faults before they become dangerous or expensive to repair.

The right way to do the job is to prepare yourself before you make a start. Wear overalls or other suitable clothing, boots and an old pair of washing-up gloves.

It is a good idea to collect the following items and only use them for cleaning your machine:

Plastic bucket
Small quantity of washing-up liquid, or a
　degreaser
A clean, soft sponge
Some clean, soft rags
Metal polish
Wax car polish
Silicone spray
Polythene bags, plus large rubber bands
An old nylon washing-up brush.

Place your machine on its main stand, on a hard surface with good drainage. Then put your polythene bags over the following: the end of the exhaust silencer, the air intake, the throttle, and the electrics. This will protect them from the water.

Starting at the front, soften the dirt with plenty of warm water, and gradually work towards the back of the machine, rubbing the dirt off with the sponge. Do not use soapy water (the soap will remove oil and grease from bearings, etc. and speed up the attack of rust), unless the dirt is very oily. In this case, only use a weak solution, using your nylon washing-up brush to reach all the awkward places. Do not forget to clean the spokes, around the carburettor and under the mudguards, as well as the main systems.

Old toothbrushes are great for reaching into all the fiddly parts.

If some parts are very oily or greasy, use a rag soaked in paraffin to remove the dirt. Do not use petrol, as it is too harsh and will damage paintwork and plastic parts, and the fumes are highly flammable. Rinse off with clean water and then dry the ma-

Do not polish disc brakes, handlebar grips, foot pegs, the seat or kick start lever

chine. You can then remove the polythene bags. When dry, apply a good wax polish to all the hard surfaces and polish to a shine.

If your machine has disc brakes, DO NOT polish them or put anything on them. It may make them look nice and shiny, but they will not work!

Rust develops quickly on bare metal, so if your bike has a scratch in the paintwork, seal it with the correct primer and paint it. Your dealer will be able to supply you with the primer and touch-up paint to match your original colour.

Finally, use a small amount of silicone spray around the engine, electrics and levers to disperse any water and to help protect the machine from moisture.

REMEMBER
Do not polish the following: disc brakes, handlebar grips, foot pegs, saddle.
A clean, well-maintained machine says a lot about you; a dirty, rusty one is often dangerous and is no credit to the rider!

Maintenance

Correct, regular maintenance by an auth-orized dealer is the key to a smooth run-

ning, reliable machine. Look after your bike and it will look after you. Between regular services, there are a number of things you must do yourself. These are all detailed in the owner's manual supplied with a new machine, or available from your dealer for a secondhand one. Look up the daily safety check and periodic maintenance.

You do not have to be a mechanic to look after your machine between services. ANYONE can cope, provided they follow the golden rules:

1 If you do not understand, or doubt your ability, contact your local dealer for advice.

2 Before starting any job, read the instruc-tions in your owner's manual or hand-book carefully.

3 Make sure that you have the correct tools (as supplied in the machine's tool kit) before you start.

4 Do not rush the job.

5 Never use pliers to grip nuts or bolts.

6 Never use force; there must be a reason for the resistance, look!

Before carrying out any maintenance, there is one task that must be carried out; clean your machine. It makes it more pleasant to work upon and will help to reveal any problems. When you have done

this, you will be ready to carry out your maintenance checks and, if necessary, adjustments. As there are so many different machines, it is impossible to give details here for your particular machine. Therefore, you will need to consult your handbook. The following is intended as a brief guide to maintenance only.

Engine oil

Four-stroke Check that the oil is at the required level, as shown on the dipstick, or in the sight glass, when the engine is cold and the bike is on its main stand on a level surface. If necessary, top up with the correct oil, taking care not to over-fill, and replace the filler cap firmly.

Two-stroke Injection system: make sure that the oil tank is topped up to the correct level with the recommended type of oil for your bike. Do not mix mineral-based oils with vegetable-based oils.

Premix system: make sure that you mix the correct ratio of oil and petrol for your bike.

When choosing oils and lubricants for your machine, ALWAYS follow the manufacturer's recommended types; there is a vast range to choose from.

When disposing of old oil, pour it into a

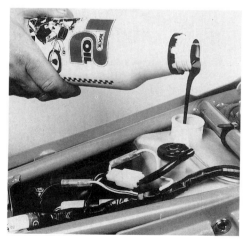

secure container and take it to a local waste disposal site that accepts used oil—not all do.

Radiator

With liquid-cooled machines, remember to keep the radiator's header tank topped up with the correct mix of distilled water and anti-freeze. Never use tap water, and make sure that you only use the anti-freeze suitable for your engine. Take care when handling anti-freeze, as it is highly poisonous and will mark paintwork if you spill it.

Battery

Carefully check that the battery's electrolyte or fluid level is between the two indicators marked on the battery casing. If necessary, top up the level with distilled water; never use tap water. Check each cell and replace the caps securely. Make sure that the battery breather pipe is connected and that it is not kinked in any way. The terminals should be clean, tight and smeared lightly with Vaseline.

Drum brakes

As the brake linings wear down in use, so the operating lever/pedal needs to be adjusted; refer to your manual or handbook. Make sure that there is a little free play before the brakes 'bite', and after adjusting, apply the lever or pedal hard several times to ensure their smooth operation. Also make sure that the brake lining wear indicator lies within the usable range. If it

Topping up the oil tank

A selection of oils and lubricants

ABOVE Top up the battery with distilled (de-ionised) water only

LEFT Keep the radiator header tank topped up. The coolant level should be kept between the marks on the side of the tank

BELOW LEFT A drum brake

does not, then the brake linings will need replacing; contact your dealer.

Having adjusted the brakes, re-adjust the brake warning light. It should be set to come on just before the brake operates. Remember that the brakes are vital to your safety. If you are unsure about making the adjustments, leave this to your dealer—better safe than sorry.

Disc brakes

Disc brakes do not need adjustment, as pad wear is automatically compensated for, but you must check frequently that the pad material is at least 1 mm thick. When it falls to this level, ask your dealer to replace the pads. Disc brakes are usually hydraulically operated; check that the fluid level is at the correct height and that

ABOVE A disc brake

LEFT Checking the tyre pressure

ABOVE RIGHT Checking tread depth, using the milled edge of a coin as a guide

RIGHT Checking tread depth, using a proper gauge

there are no leaks in the system. Take care when topping up the system. Only use the recommended type of fluid from a new container, and wipe any spillage off the paintwork immediately. Again, if you are unsure about this procedure, contact your dealer.

Tyres

The condition of the tyres is vital to keeping you on the road. Correct tyre pressures are crucial; if they are wrong, the machine's handling will be affected and you will be more likely to have a puncture. It is an offence to ride with tyre pressures substantially different to those recommended by the manufacturer.

Tyre pressures should be checked daily, and always when the tyres are cold, with a tyre pressure gauge that is known to be accurate. Always replace the tyre dust caps after checking or adjusting the pressure. The depth of tread is also important. There is a legal minimum depth of 1 mm over the tyre, but 2 mm is much safer. Below this, the tyre should be replaced. There are special depth gauges available, but as a rough guide, the raised edge of a ten pence coin is 1 mm deep.

Exhaust system

Check the exhaust system for tightness and leaks, and only use the standard exhaust for your machine. Two-stroke machines may need to have their exhausts decoked after a certain mileage, and you will need to refer to the manual for information.

Drive chain

The drive chain is one of the most hard working areas on your machine and needs constant maintenance. Lubrication is vital to the life of your chain and the smooth running of your machine.

At regular intervals, brush your chain with paraffin and allow it to dry. Then spray it with chain lubricant or engine oil. Direct the lubricant between the inner faces of the side plates and the rollers. When clean, check the adjustment of the

75

BELOW Lubricating the cables   *ABOVE Lubricating the chain*

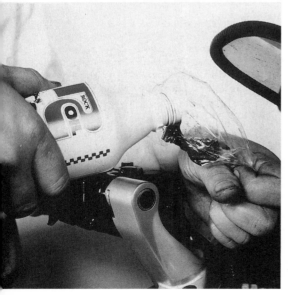

chain. Place the machine on its main stand on a level surface, then check the chain tension mid-way between the sprockets. Your machine's handbook will give you the required amount of free play. Rotate the wheel slowly and check several times to find the tightest point. Make any adjustment according to the owner's manual.

Cables
Cables should operate smoothly, and to do so, require periodic lubrication and adjustment. To lubricate a cable, remove it from the lever, and make a funnel around one end from a polythene bag, sealing it with an elastic band. Fill the funnel with light machine oil and allow it to soak down through the cable. This can be left overnight. When well lubricated, remove the funnel and wipe away any excess oil. Replace the cable and adjust it to the gap given in the owner's manual. Nylon lined

cables should only be lightly lubricated at each end. If a cable is damaged or kinked in any way, ask your dealer to replace it.

General

Remember that it is a legal requirement that all lights fitted to your machine must work. If any don't, check the connections and, if necessary, replace the bulb(s). Damaged indicators and rear lights must not be repaired with bits of coloured plastic tape.

All nuts, bolts and screws should be checked for tightness, which will ensure that nothing falls off from vibration.

Luggage

If you intend to carry any luggage on your machine, you should give careful consideration to where you are going to place it and how you are going to secure it.

On a small, light bike, it is very easy to upset the balance of the machine with too much luggage. Any load carried should be fixed firmly to the machine within the safety triangle shown below.

Some machines come fitted with luggage racks or carriers, but make sure that you know the carrying limit for these. Ask your dealer, or look it up in the machine's handbook.

Heavy loads should be carried on the petrol tank in front of the rider, and a securely-fastened tank bag is ideal. These come in a wide range of sizes and shapes. Choose one with good handles or straps that is secure on your machine, yet can be easily removed and carried around comfortably.

If you carry things on a regular basis, it is worth investing in some soft luggage, such as a tank bag or saddle bags. Choose ones that have good fittings and that can be carried on your back when removed from the bike. Expanding types of tank bag can be very useful for that unexpected parcel, or the extras that you hadn't bargained for. Check that the fittings are adequate to attach the bag firmly to your machine when it is loaded. When on the

ABOVE The safety triangle. Try to load the machine within the safety triangle, fixing the tank bag and saddle bags securely to the machine

ABOVE Tank bags

Throw-over panniers. All luggage should be firmly strapped to the machine itself

machine, the bag should hardly move, as any extra movement could allow the luggage to slide about, upsetting the machine's stability. Check also that when you are seated on the machine, the luggage does not interfere with your access to, or the operation of, any of the controls.

Ensure that the bags are securely closed before you move off. Any gap will allow air into the bag at speed, which could cause it to burst or fly open, spreading your belongings all over the road.

The rules for carrying luggage safely are:

1 Do not attempt to carry large, heavy loads on a motorcycle.

2 Make sure that any load is carried in luggage holders securely fastened to your machine.

3 NEVER carry solid articles in your clothing; they could cause severe internal injuries in an accident.

4 Make sure that any grips or fasteners are attached to solid parts of the machine, such as the frame.

5 Only buy rigid luggage, or carriers, when you have a larger machine that can cope with the load.

6 Use elasticized luggage grips (bungees) with care; they can fly off, if not securely fastened, and cause serious eye injuries.

7 Only use luggage grips with rubber-coated hooks, as these will prevent damage to your machine.

8 Check the security of your luggage each time you stop; if necessary, tighten the straps or grips.

9 Wrap any load that you carry in polythene bags (bin liners are ideal), as this will ensure that it stays dry.

10 Do not ride wearing a rucksack, or any other bag, attached to you. The higher centre of gravity will cause dangerous instability, particularly on smaller machines.

11 Remember that any load will affect the performance of your machine, so ride accordingly.

Pillion riding

Motorcycling can be even greater fun if you share it with a friend riding on the back, but to be able to do so, you must be able to meet the law's demands. You may

The correct way for a pillion rider to get on the machine

only carry a pillion passenger if you, or they, have a full motorcycle licence. In addition, your machine must have a proper seat and foot pegs for your passenger, who must also wear an approved type helmet and eye protection.

In an accident, it is often the pillion passenger who is injured, since they have nothing solid to hang on to and tend to catapult forward over the rider's back. As a rider, therefore, you must take full responsibility for your pillion passenger's safety. REMEMBER that their life is literally in your hands.

When riding with a pillion passenger, it will be different. The machine will not handle in the same way, and it will take you longer to stop. Start off nice and slowly until you are both happy. Find out first if your passenger has ridden pillion before. If they have not, explain how to get on and off the machine correctly. Explain that when you are riding, the motorcycle will not fall over when you lean it into a bend, so that they do not panic and lean in the opposite direction. Tell them that the wind pressure will not blow them off the back, that they should relax and work with you so that you can both enjoy a smooth ride. One of the fastest ways to lose a friend is to ride selfishly. It is not impressive to

frighten someone who has trusted you enough to ride on the back of your bike.

To help you enjoy riding with a pillion passenger, here are some simple tips:

1 Only carry a pillion passenger if *you* or *they* have a full motorcycle licence.

2 Your machine must have a proper seat and foot pegs for a pillion passenger.

3 Make sure that they wear an approved type helmet and eye protection.

4 Make sure that they know how to put on and securely fasten the helmet.

5 Make sure that your passenger wears sensible protective clothing; jacket, boots and gloves.

6 Make sure that they know not to get on the machine until you are ready and signal them to do so.

If you are intending to ride pillion:

1 Get on the machine by swinging a leg over, then, sitting down, raise your feet on to the foot pegs.

2 Settle into a comfortable position, hold on to the grab rail, if fitted, or the rider's hips, or your knees.

3 Look over the rider's left or right shoul-

Correctly seated pillion rider

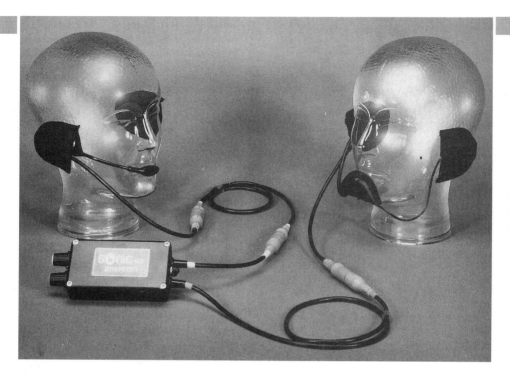

der, but do not keep changing position.

4 Remember to lean into bends with the rider.

5 Do not put your feet down at traffic lights, junctions, etc.

6 Do not make any signals for the rider.

7 Do not shift around whilst the machine is moving.

8 Relax and enjoy the ride!

Communication

With a pillion passenger, it makes it safer if you can talk to each other. Unfortunately, above 30 mph, wind noise makes it

A motorcycle intercom system

impossible to hear what is being said.

Today, it is possible to buy communication systems that make it possible for the rider and pillion passenger to talk to each other. Some are very basic and only work at speeds below 45 mph; the more expensive ones are electrical and have their own power supply. These intercoms often allow you to plug in a radio/cassette player, or even a CB radio.

Remember that your concentration will be reduced if you are holding a conversation, or you are getting carried away by rock music at full volume!

CHAPTER 7

Help!

Accident procedure

If you are ever unfortunate enough to be involved in an accident, even though no one has been injured, there is a correct procedure to be followed. The majority of people will be shaken by an accident, even a minor one, but try to remain calm and collect as much information as possible to help your insurance claim.

Informing the police

Not every accident needs to be reported to the police, but the law requires you to stop at the scene of an accident:

1 If anyone, apart from you, has been injured.
2 If any vehicle, apart from your own, has been damaged.
3 If certain animals—horse, cow, sheep, pig, dog, or goat—have been injured.
You must give your name, address and machine's registration number to anyone who has reasonable grounds for wanting them, i.e. the driver, or rider, of a vehicle you may have collided with, the owner of any property you may have damaged, etc. If serious damage has been caused, it is advisable to inform the police.

REMEMBER
Whatever happens, DO NOT ADMIT LIABILITY FOR AN ACCIDENT. If necessary, a court will decide who is to blame for an accident. You may also invalidate your insurance if you admit liability.

Try to remember the following procedure:

1 Do not admit liability.
2 Give your name, address and registration number to anyone who has reasonable grounds for wanting them.
3 Collect the names and addresses of any witnesses.
4 Draw a sketch map to show the position of any vehicles involved in the accident.
5 Before restarting your machine, move it off the road and, starting at the front, check it over carefully. Make sure that your brakes, steering, lights, etc, all work.
6 If your machine has been damaged and cannot be ridden, ask if you may leave it in someone's drive. It not, park it off the road, out of the way of any vehicles, but where it can be seen, and arrange for it to be collected.
7 Before riding after an accident, make sure that you are composed enough to ride. If you do not feel up to riding, due to shock, DON'T RIDE; catch a bus.
8 Inform your insurance company, as soon as possible, of any accident, loss or damage.

Post-accident procedure

This is a basic guide to the action that should be taken after an accident involving casualties. These notes are intended as a guide only, and further details may be obtained from a first-aid manual. If possible, practical instruction should be obtained from one of the following:

The British Red Cross Society
St John Ambulance Brigade
St Andrew's Ambulance Association

The addresses and telephone numbers of these bodies may be found in the telephone directory.

Practice will ensure that the procedure can be correctly applied if, and when, it is required. There are four main parts to the procedure, which should be followed in this order.

1 PROTECT THE ACCIDENT SCENE.

2 SUMMON THE EMERGENCY SERVICES.

3 MAKE ANY VEHICLE SAFE.

4 ATTEND TO THE CASUALTIES.

Protect the accident scene

To prevent further collisions, park any vehicles safely and turn on their lights and/or the hazard warning lights. Instruct bystanders to wave down oncoming traffic. At night, use a torch. If possible, use warning triangles, placing them at least 200 m from the accident.

DO NOT TURN YOUR BACK TO ONCOMING TRAFFIC. BE SEEN!

DO NOT STOP ON THE MOTORWAY, BUT CONTINUE TO THE NEXT EMERGENCY PHONE AND SUMMON THE EMERGENCY SERVICES.

Summon the emergency services

Send the next person to arrive at the scene of the accident to the nearest telephone to summon the emergency services. Ask them to report back to you so that you know that the emergency services are on their way. Emergency calls are free, so no coins or phonecard are required. Dial 999, state the service that you require and, when asked, give the following information:

Summon the emergency services by dialling 999

1 THE NUMBER YOU ARE CALLING FROM.

2 THE EXACT LOCATION OF THE ACCIDENT.

3 THE NUMBER OF CASUALTIES AND WHETHER ANY ARE TRAPPED.

4 ANY OTHER RELEVANT INFORMATION.

DO NOT REPLACE THE TELEPHONE RECEIVER UNTIL THE OPERATOR DOES SO. THEN REPORT BACK SO THAT PEOPLE KNOW THAT THE EMERGENCY SERVICES ARE ON THE WAY.

Make any vehicles safe

Turn off the engine of any crashed vehicle by either using the ignition switch or kill button. Apply the handbrake, engage gear and/or block the wheels so that the vehicle cannot move. Turn off the fuel.

DO NOT ALLOW ANY SMOKING IN, OR NEAR, THE CRASHED VEHICLES!

DO NOT APPROACH ANY VEHICLE DISPLAYING A HAZARD INFORMATION PANEL (refer to the Highway Code), unless you are sure that it is safe to do so.

Attend to the casualties

Always attend to the casualties who are quiet first. They are usually the most badly injured.

Do not move any casualty, unless there is a danger from fire or some other hazard.

Do not remove the helmet of an unconscious motorcyclist, unless they have stopped breathing.

If you have to remove a helmet, use two people, one to actually undo and remove the helmet carefully, the other to support the victim's head and neck. Ensure that the helmet goes with the victim to hospital so that the doctor can see the amount of damage.

If untrained, use the following simple guide.

Breathing Check any unconscious casualty for signs of breathing. If the casualty is not breathing, check that there are no obstructions in the mouth or airway.

To ensure the airway is open, support the back of the victim's neck, press the top of the head back and pull the jaw up. By doing this, the casualty may start to breathe. If they do start to breathe, check constantly for regular breathing. If not, keep the head back and pinch the casualty's nose firmly. Take a deep breath, seal your mouth around the casualty's mouth and blow steadily into their lungs

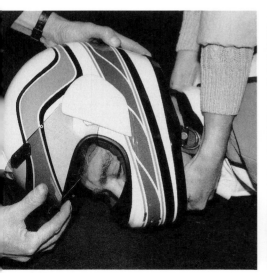

Undo the strap, tilt the helmet back and slowly lift until it is clear of the chin

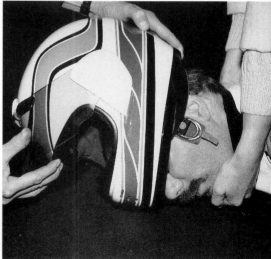

Move the helmet forward so that it passes over the base of the skull, then lift it off

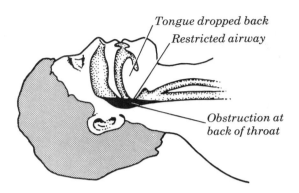

Tongue dropped back

Restricted airway

Obstruction at
back of throat

ABOVE Checking the airway

**BELOW Tilt head back to open mouth
and airway**

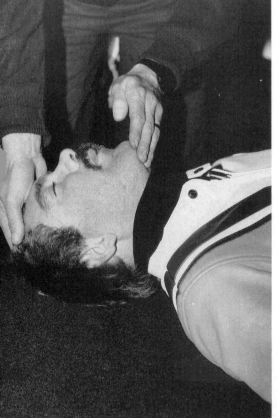

until the chest rises. Remove your mouth
and allow the chest to deflate.

Repeat this process at your normal rate
of breathing, until the casualty starts to
breathe for themselves.

Bleeding If a casualty is bleeding, this
must be stopped as soon as possible. If you
can, lower the casualty and, if there is no
sign of broken bones, raise the injured
part. Then apply and maintain pressure
over and around the wound.

DO NOT REMOVE ANY OBJECT FROM THE
WOUND.

DO NOT DISTURB ANY CLOT THAT
FORMS.

COVER THE WOUND WITH A CLEAN
DRESSING OR SUITABLE SUBSTITUTE.

Consciousness Any unconscious casualty should have been checked first for
signs of breathing and/or bleeding.

If the casualty just appears to be unconscious, loosen tight clothing at the neck,
chest and waist. Check that the air passage
is clear. Arrange for someone to stay with
the casualty to check on their breathing. If
a casualty is unconscious and there are no
signs of broken bones, they should be
placed in the coma or recovery position.

Place the casualty on their side with the
head tilted gently back. The arm and leg on

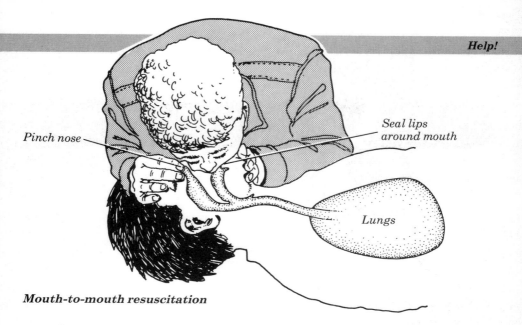

Pinch nose

Seal lips around mouth

Lungs

Mouth-to-mouth resuscitation

the side on which they are laying should be stretched out behind them. The other arm and leg should be bent in front, with the knee and elbow bent at about 90 degrees.

All of the above information is provided as a basic guide and should be supplemented by reference to a first-aid manual and, if possible, training from qualified instructors of first aid.

IF YOU ARE UNFORTUNATE ENOUGH TO BE INVOLVED IN AN ACCIDENT, FOLLOW THE POST-ACCIDENT PROCEDURE AND YOU WILL HELP TO SAVE LIFE.

The recovery position

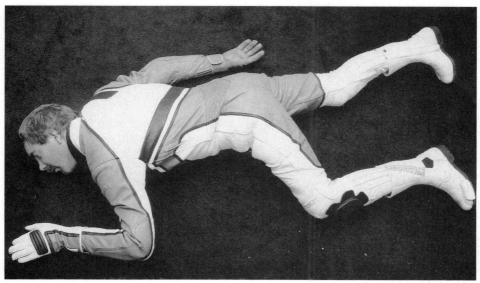

CHAPTER

8

Useful information

Motorcycle rider's organizations

These organizations run training schemes and social events, such as observed runs, rallies, discos, local meetings, etc. In addition, representations are made to government regarding motorcycle legislation.

British Motorcyclists Federation Ltd
Jack Wiley House, 129 Seaforth Avenue, Motspur Park, New Malden, Surrey
KT3 6JU.
Tel 01-942-7814

Institute of Advanced Motorists
IAM House, 359 Chiswick High Road, London W4 4HS.
Tel. 01-994 4403

Institute of Motorcycling
7 Buckingham Gate, London SW1 6JS.
Tel. 01-630-5454

Motor Cycle Action Group
PO Box 750, Birmingham B30 3BA.
Tel. 021-459 5860

Motorcycle manufacturers

There is a lot of fun to be had in owning and running a moped or motorcycle, but if things go wrong, or you need help, use the following information. Your local dealer should be able to help you with most problems. Information can also be obtained from the motorcycle press and the manufacturers or the importers.

Aprilia
Aprilia UK
USAB Ltd
Cottage Farm, Main Street, Thixendale, North Yorkshire.
Tel. 0377 88438

BMW
Ellesfield Avenue, Bracknell, Berkshire.
Tel. 0344 426565

BSA Company Ltd
Units 98/99, Norwick Park Business Centre, Blockley, nr Moreton-in-Marsh, Gloucestershire GL56 9RF.
Tel. 0386 700753

Cagiva
Moto Vecchia
Unit 5, Havenbury Estate, Station Road, Dorking, Surrey RH4 1GS.
Tel. 0306 883825

Enfield India
Bavanar Products Ltd
47 Beaumont Road, Purley, Surrey
CR2 2EJ.

Fantic
South Essex Leisure Ltd
35 High Street, Hornchurch, Essex
RM11 1RE.
Tel. 04024 58158

Garelli/Morini
Harglo Ltd
462 Station Road, Dorridge, nr Solihull, West Midlands.
Tel. 05645 5835

Gilera
Bob Wright Motorcycles
4 Orchard Street, Weston-super-Mare,
BS23 1RQ.
Tel. 0934 413847

Harley-Davidson
Harley-Davidson International
PO Box 79, Northampton NN3 5HX.
Tel. 0604 414876

Honda
Honda UK Ltd
4 Power Road, Chiswick, London W4 5YT.
Tel. 01-747 1400

Husqvarna
Pro-Circuit UK Ltd
Unit M, Bumper Farm Industrial Estate,
Chippenham, Wiltshire.
Tel. 0249 656547

Jawa-CZ
Skoda (GB) Ltd
Bergen Way, North Lynn Industrial
Estate, King's Lynn, Norfolk.
Tel. 0537 61176

Kawasaki
Kawasaki Motors (UK) Ltd
1 Dukes Meadow, Millboard Road,
Bourne End, Buckinghamshire SL8 5XF.
Tel. 0628 851000

KTM
Brian Goss Motorcycles
31 Oxford Road, Pen Mill Trading Estate,
Yeovil, Somerset.
Tel. 0935 72424

Laverda/Moto Guzzi
Laverda Concessionaires (UK) Ltd
Woolsbridge Industrial Estate, 6 Old Barn
Farm Road, Three Legged Cross,
Wimborne, Dorset.
Tel. 0202 824531/2/3

Maico
Bill Brown Motorcycles
High Street, Whitehaven, Cumbria.
Tel. 0946 2697

Montesa
Jim Sandiford Motorcycles Ltd
30/38 Walmersley Road, Bury,
Lancashire.
Tel. 061-764 8204

Morini
See Garelli

Moto Guzzi
See Laverda

MZ and Zebretta
Wilf Green Ltd
MZ House, New Street, Halfway,
nr Sheffield.
Tel. 0742 488500

Norton
Norton Motors Ltd
Lynn Lane, Shenstone, nr Lichfield,
Staffordshire WS14 0EA.
Tel. 0543 480101

Puch Steyr
Moore Large & Co. Ltd
Gothic House, Barkergate, Nottingham.
Tel. 0602 506522

Suzuki
Heron Suzuki (GB) Ltd
46–62 Gatwick Road, Crawley, West
Sussex RH10 2XF.
Tel. 0293 518000

Tomos
Tomos Netherland BV
44–46 Stocks Street, Manchester M8 8QG.
Tel. 061-834 6117

Velo-Solex
Moto-Vation
300 Old Kent Road, London SE1 5UE.
Tel. 01-703 7881

Vespa
Vespa UK Ltd
See Heron Suzuki

Yamaha
Mitsui Machinery Sales Ltd
Oakcroft Road, Chessington, Surrey
KT9 1SA.
Tel. 01-397 5111

Sport

Amateur Motorcycle Association
Darlaston Road, Walsall, Staffordshire
WS2 9XL.
Tel. 0922 39517

Association of Road Racing Clubs
11 Turnpike Drive, Water Orton,
Birmingham B46 1PP.
Tel. 021-749 2277

Autocycle Union
Millbuck House, Corporation Street,
Rugby, Warwickshire CV21 2DN.
Tel. 0788 70332

British Drag Racing Association
Bakersfield, 29 West Drive, Caldercote,
Cambridgeshire CB3 7NY.
Tel. 0954 210028

British Schoolboy Motorcycle
Association
18 Glenpark Crescent, Kingscourt,
Stroud, Gloucestershire.
Tel. 04536 6516

Motor Cycle Union of Ireland
47 Beechill Park West, Belfast BT8 4NW.
Tel. 0232 703004

National Sprint Association
51 Hale Street, Warrington, Cheshire
WA2 7PM.
Tel. 0925 573093

Quad Racing Information Service
Red Cat Racing
Gelding Park Raceway, Small Dole,
Sussex BN5 9XH.
Tel. 0903 816454

Scottish Auto-cycle Union
Kippilaw, Longridge Road, Whitburn,
West Lothian EH47 0LG.
Tel. 0501 42663

Trial Riders Fellowship
197 Britten Road, Brighton Hill,
Basingstoke, Hampshire RG22 4HW.
Tel. 0256 841350

Youth Motorcycle Sport Association
20 Kensington Gardens, Ilkeston,
Derbyshire.
Tel. 0602 328989

The trade associations

There are four motorcycle trade associations who support the Office of Fair Trading's Code of Practice. Contact the relevant trade association if you have a problem with one of their dealers that cannot be resolved. Don't forget that they can do nothing unless the dealer is a member of their association.

Motor Cycle Association (MCA)
Starley House, Eaton Road, Coventry
CV1 2FH.
Tel. 0203 227427
For any complaints about new bikes

The Conciliation Service
Motor Agents Association Ltd
73 Park Street, Bristol BS1 5PS.
For complaints about member dealers

Motorcycle Retailers Association
31A High Street, Tunbridge Wells, Kent
TN1 1XN.

REMEMBER
Some traders may belong to more than one of these associations. Don't make a complaint to more than one association at a time. Also, don't contact the trader or manufacturer and the trade association at the same time—this could cause confusion and, therefore, delay. Keep a copy of all letters or correspondence that you send or that you receive.

Owners clubs

Honda Owners Club
4 Kingsbridge Road,
172 Lordship Road, London N16 5HB.
Tel. 0802 2026

Italian Motorcycle Club
48 Whitny Avenue, Stockton Lane, York
YO3 0ET.
Tel. 0904 414407

Norton Owners Club
53M Oak Way, Feltham TW14 8AT.

Suzuki Owners Club
c/o Phil Hingert, 46 Lorne Street,
Burslem, Stoke on Trent, ST6 1AR.

Yamaha Owners Club
c/o Mitsui Machinery Sales, Oakcroft
Road, Chessington, Surrey KT9 1JA.

There are many motorcycle clubs covering
a wide range of interests, and details of
their events often appear in the motorcycle
press.

Motoring organizations

Automobile Association
Fanum House, Basingstoke, Hants RG21
2EA.
Tel. 0256 493031

Royal Automobile Club
Motoring Services Ltd
PO Box 100, RAC House, Lansdowne
Road, Croydon CR9 2JA.
Tel. 01-464 5091

National Breakdown Rider Rescue
PO Box 300, Leeds LS99 2LZ.
Tel. 0532 393666

Europ Assistance
252 High Street, Croydon, Surrey
CR10 1NF.
Tel. 01-680 1234

Autohome Recovery Club
202–204 Kettering Road, Northampton
NN1 4HE.
Tel. 0604 28730

Britannia Recovery
Byram House, 22 Byram Street,
Huddersfield, West Yorkshire HD1 1DY.
Tel. 0484 514848

By joining one of these organizations, you
will have the peace of mind of knowing
that if you break down on the road, you can
get some help to get home.

Papers and magazines

There are a number of newspapers and
magazines catering for most types of
motoring. They provide news, information
and advertising by dealers, accessory
shops, clothing manufacturers, book sup-
pliers, event organizers etc.

Motor Cycle News/Bike Magazine/Dirt
Bike Rider/Classic Bike/Motorcycle
Mechanics/Motorcycle Racer/What
Bike/Performance Bikes
EMAP Publications Ltd
13 Holkham Road, Orton Southgate,
Peterborough PE2 0UF.
Tel. 0733 237111

Motor Cycle International
Advanced Publishing Ltd
21 Paul Street, London EC2A 4LB.
Tel. 01-729 3922

Trials and Motocross News
Lancaster and Morecambe Newspapers
Morecambe, Lancashire LA4 4AG.
Tel. 0524 414531

Motorcycle and Workshop
Trowley Bottom Publishing
Flamstead, St Albans AL3 8EE.
Tel. 0582 842381/2

Motorcycle shows

Throughout the year, a number of shows
take place, some general, others of a spec-
ialized nature. The following are just
examples. Details of dates, times, venues,
prices, etc. will be found in the motorcycle
press.

The International Bike Show
Earls Court, London
(usually early in October)

The Bristol Dirt Bike Show
Bristol
(usually 11–13 December)

The Classic Motorcycle Show
Sandown Exhibition Centre
The Racecourse, Esher, Surrey.
Enquiries 0272 650465
(usually mid-November)

Museums

Motorcycles have been around for about
100 years, and there have been many
changes. The following museums have
examples of those changes.

The National Motorcycle Museum
Bogay Hall, Henwood Lane, Catherine-de-
Barnes, Solihull, West Midlands B91 2TH.
Tel. 021-704 2784

Beaulieu Motor Museum
George Montague Building, Beaulieu,
Hampshire SO42 7ZN.
Tel. 0590 612345

Sammy Miller Classic Motorcycle
Museum
New Milford, Hampshire.

Forms

Getting the right form can be a problem; a
simple point to remember is that most of
the forms relate to the driver. These forms
have the prefix 'D', but if they refer to the
vehicle, they have the prefix 'V'.

The list below gives some of the most
common forms that you might need, and
also tells you where you can get them.

Form	Purpose	From
D1	Driving licence application form	LPO
D100	What you need to know about driver licensing	LPO
D123MC	Certificate of passing Part One test	ATC
DL24	Statement of Failure	AEX
DL26	Application for a driving test appointment	LPO/TAO
DL26(W)	As above, but the test is conducted in Welsh	LPO/TAO
DL68	Your Driving Test, a booklet of information about the driving test	DVLC
V10	Application for a vehicle licence	LPO/LVLO
V14	Refund application on return of vehicle excise	LPO/LVLO
V20	Application for duplicate vehicle excise licence	LPO/LVLO
V55	Vehicle registration document application form	D/LVLO/DVLC
V62	Application for registration document	LPO/LVLO
V100	Registering and Licensing your motor vehicle, some notes to help you	LPO/LVLO

DVLC	Driver and Vehicle Licensing Centre
LPO	Licensing Post Office (usually main Post Office)
ATC	Approved Training Centre
TAO	Traffic Area Office
AEX	Approved Examiner
D	Dealer
LVLO	Local Vehicle Licensing Office

For further help, contact:

Driver Enquiry Unit
Driver and Vehicle Licensing Centre
(DVLC), Swansea SA6 7JL.
Tel. 0792 72151
Please quote your driver number.

Vehicle Enquiry Unit
DVLC, Swansea, SA99 1BL.
(Note post code)
Tel. 0792 72134

Local Vehicle Licensing Office
Address and phone number can be found in
the phone book under 'Transport, Department of'.

Traffic Area Office
Address and phone number can be found in
the phone book under 'Transport, Department of'.

REMEMBER

Read forms carefully before you begin to
fill them in.

Write clearly, using black ink and block
letters.

Give your driver number when enquiring
about driver-related matters.

Give the vehicle registration number when
enquiring about vehicle-related matters.

Use your post code.

Check through the form before posting.

Use the correct address, including the post
code.

Glossary

AA—Automobile Association; motoring organization offers rescue, breakdown service, legal and technical advice, etc.

ABS—Anti-lock Brake System. A brake safety system that prevents the wheel locking and causing a skid.

ACU—Auto Cycle Union, the governing body of motorcycle sport in the UK.

Additives—Chemicals added to oil, petrol, etc, to give special qualities.

Air filter—A device to clean the air of dust and airborne particles before it enters and damages the carburettor. Also known as air cleaner.

Alternator—Electrical generator powered by the engine that produces an alternating current (AC) supply.

Anti-dive—Device fitted to the front of a machine, usually brake-activated, that stops the machine dipping or diving whilst under braking.

Anti-freeze—Chemical mixture added to the cooling system to prevent freezing of coolant.

Anti-mist—Chemical spray used to prevent misting or fogging on visors. Washing-up liquid can be used as a substitute.

Battery—An electrical storage system, usually 12 volts or 6 volts.

Balaclava—Head covering, made from cotton or silk, helps keep in warmth and protects helmet lining from soiling.

Belt drive—Form of final transmission that uses a very strong belt, rather than a chain. Advantages are that it is quieter and requires far less maintenance. Kawasaki 305, Harley-Davidson use belt drive.

Bike—Slang term for a motorcycle.

Biker—Slang term for a motorcyclist.

Body armour—Protective pads and guards for use in, or under, clothing to protect joints, etc, from injury.

Bore—Inside of engine cylinder, or its diameter.

Braking distance—Distance covered between the time you apply the brakes and actually stopping. This, plus your thinking distance, will add up to your overall stopping distance.

Bronze course—Basic motorcycle training course operated by Star Rider.

Bump start—Emergency-only method of starting a motorcycle. This should only be used if the machine cannot be started by any other method. It should be done on a road without traffic about, using the following procedure.

1 Turn on the fuel and the ignition.

2 Put the machine into second or third gear.

3 Make sure that you are wearing a helmet and protective clothing.

4 Pull in the clutch and start to push your machine forward as fast as you can.

5 When you are travelling at a brisk pace, jump on to your machine and release the clutch at the same time. As the engine starts, operate the clutch and use the throttle to keep the engine running.

If possible, get someone to push you whilst you are sitting on the machine. YOU CANNOT BUMP START A MACHINE WITH AUTOMATIC TRANSMISSION

cc—Cylinder capacity of an engine, measured in cubic centimetres, i.e. 50 cc,

100 cc, 125 cc, 500 cc, etc.

Carburettor—Device that carries out the mixing of petrol and air, turning it into a fine explosive mist. The mixture is drawn into the cylinder, where a spark from the spark plug ignites it.

Chain—Form of transmission, common to most motorcycles.

Choke—Part of the carburettor, used to restrict, or choke the air supply. The richer (more fuel) mixture makes the engine easier to start when cold. Remember to turn the choke off when the engine has warmed up and is running smoothly. Do not ride with the choke on.

Clip-ons—Aftermarket handlebars. Sport, or ace, bars lower the handlebar position; ape bars raise the position.

Clutch—The clutch mechanism allows you to smoothly separate the power of the engine from the gearbox, or apply the power again, change gear or stop without stalling the engine.

Cold planing—Method used by road repairers. The surface is scraped away to leave deep grooves, often at a diagonal, that presents an extremely hazardous surface for motorcyclists.

Contact breakers—Mechanically operated switch. Part of the ignition system that causes a rapid break of current to the ignition coil and subsequently causes a spark at the sparking plug.

Conspicuity—Materials that make the rider more visible in all conditions.

Cooling—Means by which the engine is kept within its best operating temperature. Cooling can be by air, liquid or oil.

Crash bars—Add-on protective bars, i.e. engine protectors, leg protectors.

Cross-ply—Type of tyre construction, where cords are laid diagonally to the circumference of the tyre.

Cylinder—The part of the engine where the mixture is ignited, driving the piston down, then up and so producing power. A machine may have a single-, twin-, triple-, four- or even a six-cylinder engine.

Disc brake—Type of brake using a revolving metal disc that brake pads operate

against. The brake pads may produce asbestos dust; avoid contact or inhaling.

Drum brake—Type of brake using curved brake shoes that push out against the walls of a brake drum forming the hub of the wheel. The brake shoes produce asbestos dust; avoid contact or inhaling.

Exhaust—Complete exhaust/silencer system. These must now comply with and be stamped, BSAU193.

Exhaust pipe—Pipe carrying hot exhaust gases away from the engine.

Expansion chamber—Part of the exhaust silencer where gases are allowed to expand and circulate around baffles to reduce their noise level.

Fairing—Device fitted as standard, or as an add-on, to reduce drag or wind resistance.

Frame—The frame is the support for the rest of the machine's systems.

Four-stroke—Type of engine, so called because it takes four strokes of the piston to produce one power stroke. The flow of petrol/air mixture and exhaust gas is controlled by a series of valves making the four-stroke engine more complex than the two-stroke.

Gearbox—The gearbox contains a series of toothed wheels that are used to regulate the turning power of the engine to the rear wheel.

Generator—Device for producing electricity by converting rotational movement into electrical power.

Highway Code—A code for all road users, issued by the Department of the Environment, sold in HMSO bookshops and most other good bookshops.

High-tension lead—HT lead carries high-voltage current (15,000 volts plus) between the coil and the spark plug.

HT coil—Electrical device that boosts low-voltage current, 6 or 12 volts, up to high-voltage current.

Horn—Audible warning device used to let other road users know you are there.

Intercom—Device enabling rider to talk/listen to passenger, radio, cassette player or CB radio whilst on the move.

93

Kick start lever—Means of starting the engine.

Kill button—Switch located on the handlebars and operating as an 'emergency' stop for the ignition system. The switch should not be used to routinely switch off the engine.

Leathers—Term given to describe motorcycle clothing made from leather, goatskin, steer hide, horse hide or pigskin, such as jacket, jeans and one-piece or two-piece suits.

L-plates—Identifying plates to show that you are learning to ride. These plates should be clearly displayed at the front and rear of the machine at all times. The plates measure 7 in. by 7 in. and must not be cut down in size or wrapped around a fork leg.

Lifesaver—Final rearwards observation made just before making a turn.

Log book—Old name given to the vehicle registration document.

Lubrication—Means of reducing friction between moving metal parts.

Moped—Machine restricted to a maximum speed of 30 mph, weighing less than 250 kg with an engine capacity of less than 50 cc.

Motocross—Motorcycle sport, very tough cross-country racing. Riders heavily-protected by body armour.

Night riding—Riding at night requires increased concentration and conspicuity. See Chapter 6.

No claim bonus—Discount granted by insurance company for not making a claim during the previous 12 months of a policy, usually a maximum of $33\frac{1}{3}$ per cent.

Observations—Visual check to gather as much information as possible about the road surface, other road users' movements, surroundings and potential hazards.

Oil—Vital component in an engine, carrying out the following functions:
Lubrication
Cooling
Prevention of corrosion
Removal of debris from combustion

Sealing hot gases.

Oil cooler—Device that is used to cool the engine's oil.

Oversuit—Waterproof or weatherproof suit, made to be worn over protective clothing. Lightweight suits are made for summer use, and lined, heavy-weight suits are produced for winter use.

Owner's handbook/manual—Book of details about a particular machine. Contains information such as layout of controls, starting and running procedures, routine maintenance tasks, service schedules, etc.

Panniers—Type of motorcycle luggage.

Pillion passenger—Passenger carried on a motorcycle. The rider or passenger must have a full motorcycle licence, the machine must have a proper seat and foot pegs, and the passenger must also wear an approved type helmet and eye protection.

Piston—Engine component that moves up and down inside the cylinder under power.

Policy—The agreement drawn up between you and the insurance company, a contract giving the details of cover and conditions.

Polycarbonate—Type of plastic used to make the shell of a helmet.

Premium—The cost of your insurance.

Provisional licence—Temporary licence.

Radial—Type of tyre construction using perpendicular cords from the rim; the softer side walls give a lower profile or tyre height.

Reaction time—Time taken from seeing a hazard to actually applying the brakes.

Reflective material—Material able to throw back light shone upon it.

Retro-reflective—Highly reflective material, particularly effective at night.

Rev-counter—Mechanical or electrical device used to show the revolutions of the engine.

Road racing—Type of motorcycle racing held on specially closed sections of road, i.e. the Isle of Man TT, or on specially-built circuits, such as Brands Hatch.

Roadcraft—Skills required to ride or

drive safely on the road.

Rotary engine—Engine producing power from rotational movement, rather than up and down (reciprocating).

Saddle bags—Form of luggage for motorcycles.

Scrambling—Cross-country racing, now known as motocross.

Shaft drive—Form of power transmission, where a revolving shaft turns the back wheel.

Shock absorber—Type of suspension designed to absorb shocks from the road surface.

Sidecar—Attachment for carrying extra passengers.

Silencer—Part of the exhaust where noise is reduced, sometimes referred to as the muffler.

Skid—Loss of control, caused by a wheel locking. It stops turning, loosing its grip and sliding across the surface.

Slick—A racing type of tyre having no tread pattern. Grip comes from the soft make-up of the tyre. Such tyres give no grip on wet surfaces and are illegal for road use.

Snell Foundation—American safety foundation, similar to the British Standards Institute.

Sparking plug—High-voltage device producing a spark to ignite the fuel/air mixture in the cylinder.

Speedway—Type of motorcycle racing carried out on closed circuits with a shale surface, the machines have no brakes and the riders slide them around the corners.

Sprint—Type of racing where machines are raced against each other, or the clock, over a short, straight-line distance.

Sprocket—Toothed wheel connected to engine that turns the back wheel sprocket via a chain.

Steering damper—A device used to slow down the movement of the steering.

Suppressor—Electrical resistor that prevents interference from high-voltage ignition components affecting radio and television reception.

Suspension—The system supporting the machine and helping reduce the shock from surface bumps.

Swinging arm—A form of rear suspension.

Synthetic oil—Chemically-formulated oils.

Tachometer—Correct term for the rev-counter.

Tank bag—Motorcycle luggage.

Throttle—Device controlling the carburettor and, therefore, the engine output as road speed.

Tool kit—Collection of tools, usually supplied with the machine so that basic maintenance tasks can be carried out.

Top box—A rigid container fastened to the rear of the machine.

Torque—The turning power of the engine.

Touring—Long distance riding.

Trail bike—A type of bike that can be used both on- and off-road.

Training—Good motorcyclists are trained. To help you at various stages, there are a number of training schemes.

Transmission—System that connects the power from the engine to the rear wheel.

Tread—The drainage grooves cut into a tyre so that it can grip the surface in wet or damp conditions.

Trials—Cross-country riding over difficult ground requiring good machine control.

Tuning—Preparation of machine to the best of its performance.

Turbocharging—A means of using exhaust gases to drive a turbine that forces fuel into the combustion chamber under pressure. This results in an increase in power.

Two-stroke—Engine where every second stroke of the piston is a power stroke.

Visor—Eye shield fitted to the helmet, must now comply with BSI regulations BS4110.

Wankel engine—The rotary engine.